There is nothing more important success, and spiritual growth of th parents feel secure in a culture that seems to be moving from Christian values, if not openly opposing them? *The Daniel Prayer for Parents* draws from the biblical account of Daniel and his fellow captives as they not only survived but also thrived in an environment that could not have been more antagonistic. Daniel's secrets to success will teach parents how to pray for their children as they walk through the challenging developmental years of life. Parents will learn key principles to pray for their child in the important areas of health, educational excellence and development, acceptance of Christ and resolve to serve God, favor, promotion, and influence.

It's time parents stop losing their kids to the temptations and pressures of this world and start raising young men and women who set the standard of godly, successful influencers who inspire change in their surroundings.

Pastor Sawyer has given his life to reaching families through a church that has touched thousands. He is a leader among leaders. This book is a must-read for those who desire to raise successful, godly children in a culture that pulls in the opposite direction.

—Tommy Barnett
Pastor, Phoenix First
Founder, Los Angeles and Phoenix Dream Centers

I am so excited about *The Daniel Prayer for Parents* by my friend George Sawyer. I want to tell you something: parents need information when it comes to dealing with their kids, and when the rubber meets the road they need to know how to pray for them! Sometimes people pray as if they're throwing words around to see where they may splatter, without any real thought or meaning. But we have to be real specific in our prayers, especially with our children. Why? Because their future is in our hands. This book is a revelation and one that you'll go to again and again for help with your children no matter how young or old they are. Get ready to be blessed. Your life and your children's lives will never be the same!

—DR. JESSE DUPLANTIS
JESSE DUPLANTIS MINISTRIES

The Daniel Prayer for Parents is a must-read for every parent, grandparent, and guardian of this generation! If ever there was a book written for such a time as this, it is this one. My dear friend and mentor Pastor George Sawyer has written a message of hope, freedom, and authority that will awaken homes all over the world. This book will restore your fire for God just as the prayer of Daniel was birthed in the fire. We must see God invade our homes and restore truth to this generation. Parents, you can't do it alone. God's Word declares, "Unless the LORD builds the house, the builders labor in vain" (Ps. 127:1). This book is destined be a classic! I warn you that if you read the book and begin to pray the "Daniel Prayer," you need to be prepared for the results! Your home will never be the same! It is time we take our children back from the culture that desires to seduce and reduce them! This is your moment to rise up and lead! Thank you, Pastor George Sawyer, for hearing from God!

Get this book!

—PATRICK SCHATZLINE
REMNANT MINISTRIES, INTERNATIONAL
AUTHOR, *WHY IS GOD SO MAD AT ME?*,
I AM REMNANT, AND *UNQUALIFIED*

Parents cannot underestimate the potential of the prayers that they've spoken over their children. Rather than allow this culture to define their children, parents can learn the secrets to success that Daniel understood when facing the challenges of a hostile culture. More and more, America is turning from the foundational truths of Judeo-Christian values and into a secularized society, even demonstrating antipathy toward Christianity. This timely message, *The Daniel Prayer for Parents*, will empower you to know what to pray specifically and how to pray effectively so that your children will not only survive but also thrive in Babylon.

—NEIL KENNEDY
AUTHOR AND FOUNDER, FIVESTARMAN

As parents there is nothing more important to us than our children's futures. Pastor Sawyer's insight on prayer and its impact on their destinies is like a breath of fresh air. I highly recommend it.

—Jay Haizlip
Founder and senior pastor, The Sanctuary

THE

DANIEL PRAYER

for PARENTS

GEORGE SAWYER

CHARISMA
HOUSE

Most CHARISMA HOUSE BOOK GROUP products are available at special quantity discounts for bulk purchase for sales promotions, premiums, fund-raising, and educational needs. For details, write Charisma House Book Group, 600 Rinehart Road, Lake Mary, Florida 32746, or telephone (407) 333-0600.

THE DANIEL PRAYER FOR PARENTS by George Sawyer
Published by Charisma House
Charisma Media/Charisma House Book Group
600 Rinehart Road
Lake Mary, Florida 32746
www.charismahouse.com

This book or parts thereof may not be reproduced in any form, stored in a retrieval system, or transmitted in any form by any means—electronic, mechanical, photocopy, recording, or otherwise—without prior written permission of the publisher, except as provided by United States of America copyright law.

Unless otherwise noted, all Scripture quotations are taken from the Holy Bible, New International Version®, NIV®. Copyright © 1973, 1978, 1984, 2011 by Biblica, Inc.™ Used by permission of Zondervan. All rights reserved worldwide. www.zondervan.com The "NIV" and "New International Version" are trademarks registered in the United States Patent and Trademark Office by Biblica, Inc.™

Scripture quotations marked HCSB are taken from the Holman Christian Standard Bible®, Copyright © 1999, 2000, 2002, 2003, 2009 by Holman Bible Publishers. Used by permission. Holman Christian Standard Bible®, Holman CSB®, and HCSB® are federally registered trademarks of Holman Bible Publishers.

Scripture quotations marked KJV are from the King James Version of the Bible.

Scripture quotations marked MEV are taken from the Modern English Version. Copyright © 2014 by Military Bible Association. Used by permission. All rights reserved.

Scripture quotations marked NKJV are taken from the New King James Version®. Copyright © 1982 by Thomas Nelson. Used by permission. All rights reserved.

Copyright © 2015 by George Sawyer
All rights reserved

Cover design by Vincent Pirozzi
Design Director: Justin Evans

Visit the author's website at www.georgesawyer.org.

Library of Congress Cataloging-in-Publication Data:
Sawyer, George.
  The Daniel prayer for parents / by George Sawyer. -- First edition.
     pages cm

Includes bibliographical references and index.
ISBN 978-1-62998-243-4 (trade paper : alk. paper) --
ISBN 978-1-62998-244-1 (e-book)
1. Parents--Religious life. 2. Intercessory prayer--
Christianity. 3. Prayer--Christianity. 4. Daniel (Biblical
figure) I. Title.
BV4529.S37 2015
248.8′45--dc23

2015020199

While the author has made every effort to provide accurate
Internet addresses at the time of publication, neither the
publisher nor the author assumes any responsibility for
errors or for changes that occur after publication.

This publication is translated in Spanish under the title
La oración de Daniel para los padres, copyright © 2015 by
George Sawyer, published by Casa Creación, a Charisma
Media company. All rights reserved.

First edition

15 16 17 18 19 — 987654321
Printed in the United States of America

DEDICATION

WITH MY DEEPEST gratitude, I dedicate this book to those whose prayers have impacted and shaped my life. There is no one I have heard pray more often and more faithfully than my wife, Phyllis. Every day of our marriage I have been encouraged by the sound of her passion for God and His purposes for our family and His church. She has been my prayer partner for my biggest dreams and has held my hand as we have walked through the valley of the shadow of death. Phyllis, you are a prayer role model for me, and I could not love you or admire you more!

But long before I met my wife, the very first "pray-ers" who impacted my life were my mother and father. They prayed for me every day of my life. I am the man I am today because of their love, their godly example, and their unceasing prayers. They "prayed me through" the years when I was running from God. And they prayed for me when I refused to pray. I owe my life to the power of a parent's prayer.

One of my earliest memories of prayer involves my father. In the small church in which I grew up, the service always ended with everyone going forward to kneel and pray. This was not my favorite church moment. It was hard for me to be still, and I was young and could say everything I thought God may need to hear in about thirty seconds. But I always went forward and knelt beside my father. I remember watching his face and listening to his voice as he prayed. Even then I realized that my father knew God in a way that was very real and worth discovering for myself.

I learned more about prayer and God kneeling beside my father than from most of the theology courses I have taken. My father is in heaven today, yet I am convinced that I am still benefiting from his prayers even now.

My mother was saved before my father, and her prayers brought him to Christ. She paved the way. And she continues to faithfully enforce and enlarge the prayer legacy of our family.

Thanks, Mom and Dad. I owe you big time.

CONTENTS

ACKNOWLEDGMENTS

I WOULD LIKE TO thank Teresa Hana for her tireless assistance in the preparation of this book. Thanks for your encouragement and belief in *The Daniel Prayer for Parents*. I also want to thank the pastors and staff at Calvary for your encouragement and support during this project.

I want to thank Adrienne Gaines and everyone who was so great to work with at Charisma House. I pray that together we will be able to impact a generation by inspiring those who pray for them. Thanks also to Pat Schatzline for introducing me to the Charisma House family.

Last but certainly not least, I want to thank my wife, Phyllis, and my family for sharing our time and for believing in me and the message of *The Daniel Prayer for Parents*.

INTRODUCTION

IT WAS THE Sunday before the new school year was to begin. I had no idea that what we would do on this day was so important it would demand that we shift the order of our service and enlist our entire church family in its exercise. On this day we called to the front of our worship center every student from preschool through college—and we prayed.

For some time we had begun every school year by praying for our students. The prayer time was always very powerful and effective. But on this day something was different. I had recently concluded a message series on the life of Daniel, and what I initially thought to be an interesting collateral blessing of the study would forever transform the way our congregation would pray for our children and students.

While I was studying Daniel's incredible life for that sermon series, I sensed God directing me to Daniel chapter 1 as I prayed for my own children and grandchildren. There God revealed to me a very clear, intentional, and anointed prayer to speak over them every day as they were in school. I had begun praying this prayer over my own family, but on this "Back to School" Sunday, I publicly prayed my "Daniel prayer" over all these students as our church family joined me in intercession.

Something shifted spiritually in that moment. What I had been learning about the power of this prayer in my personal devotion was released that day on all of the students.

God met us. The students knew it, and so did their families. The confidence and boldness produced by this Holy Spirit-empowered, biblically based prayer was undeniable. Parents and grandparents immediately began to ask me to put the prayer in print so they could pray it daily over their students.

And so an exciting, sometimes challenging prayer journey began for the Calvary Assembly family. As you read this book, you will not only learn the dynamic principles we gleaned about how to pray for our children and students, you will also read stories of how God has wonderfully responded with unmistakable answers to our prayers for those we love.

The first day of kindergarten, the first day of middle school, the first day of high school, and even the day your "child" drives away to enter college—what do you do? How do you let go at each of these milestones? You had better learn how to pray. And not just any kind of prayer. Not prayers in which you're merely hoping, wishing, or even begging God to "do something." You must learn to pray so that your intercession defines your children's destiny and their generation as a result.

I hope that as you read this book, you do not think of this prayer as a simple formula to merely recite over your children. I pray you will come to understand and apply the truths contained within it. If you pray these principles in faith, with the understanding that God can and wants to move in your child's life, trust me, you'll be amazed at the results.

Are you ready? Let's get started.

PART 1

LAYING THE FOUNDATION

Chapter 1

YOUR PRAYERS MAKE
A DIFFERENCE

*In the third year of the reign of Jehoiakim king
of Judah, Nebuchadnezzar king of Babylon
came to Jerusalem and besieged it.*

—DANIEL 1:1, MEV

Two worlds collided, and all sense of pre-existing order was undone. To the young people tossed into this chaos, these people and their customs were strange and unfamiliar. There were new faces, new names, new sights and sounds, new pressures and influences. But this culture was not just *different*; in many ways it stood in stark contrast—even opposition—to everything the young people had been taught in their homes.

What is happening here? At the beginning of the Book of Daniel, the nation of Israel had been on a long, steady downward march away from their God and His Word. Eventually their rebellion and disregard for God had permeated their government, religion, and society at large, and God could no longer bless or protect them. Eventually they found themselves in captivity, reaping the consequences of what they had long been sowing.

Once revered, the nation had become easy prey. The armies of Babylon marched onto their fair land and into their seemingly unassailable capital city. They destroyed

1

and burned every symbol of Israel's security and faith, and looted everything of monetary value. They would even capture some of the leading citizens of Judah and cruelly march their "spoils of war" all the way back to Babylon in a parade of defeat and disgrace.

But that was not the end of Babylon's plans for these captives.

> Then the king ordered Ashpenaz, chief of his court officials, to bring into the king's service some of the Israelites from the royal family and the nobility— young men without any physical defect, handsome, showing aptitude for every kind of learning, well informed, quick to understand, and qualified to serve in the king's palace. He was to teach them the language and literature of the Babylonians.
>
> —DANIEL 1:3–4

The Babylonians wanted to train Israel's best and brightest to serve their nation, a nation steeped in idolatry and with no understanding of the one true God. The young men they handpicked showed aptitude for every kind of learning; they were intelligent and gifted. And the Babylonians wanted to misdirect their gifts and abilities to put them in service to their own ungodly kingdom. Their plan was to teach them the language, literature, customs, and purposes of Babylon, and have them forget about, or at least disregard, their God.

But there was no way these young Israelites could reach their full potential if they became disconnected from the One who gave them their gifts and talents in the first place. To live life at its highest level, we must personally know the gracious God who created us. We must realize that our talents and gifts are from God and meant to be used to serve His purposes. So what were these young Hebrews to do?

It is no accident that the Babylonians targeted the young for their training plan. Satan constantly seeks as his victims the most vulnerable, the young, the least able to defend themselves. And why? He wants to attack and destroy their dreams, hopes, and God-given potential before they have the opportunity to develop.

Satan is always more afraid of a person's future than his past! Every generation is born with a death assignment from Satan and a life-more-abundantly assignment from God. This is why we must pray for this rising generation.

There has always existed a hellish strategy to crush a dream before it develops, to exterminate deliverance as soon as it is birthed from the womb of God's design. Think with me of Moses. He was born in a crisis, in a pivotal moment in time, as God's answer to His people's prayers for deliverance. But if Pharaoh had his way, Moses would never have been born.

In a plan that could only have been demonically inspired, Pharaoh issued a death decree that all the male babies born to the enslaved Israelites must be executed at birth. Yet with great love and courage, Moses's parents refused to obey Pharaoh's decree. We know the rest of the story. Moses left an incredible legacy—and it was all because his parents protected their son and trusted God with his future.

Fast-forward to two thousand years ago. God came to deliver us from the power of sin. Jesus Christ was born of a virgin in a nondescript stable in Bethlehem. The perfect God allowed His divinity to be clothed with humanity.

When this happened, an alarm went off in hell, and Satan once again found a human puppet through which he could attack this young deliverer. Herod, as Pharaoh before him, decreed that the male babies of Israel must be put to death at birth. Why? Satan wanted to exterminate the Deliverer before Jesus could accomplish the purpose for which God put Him on this earth.

First Moses, then Jesus—and Satan still hasn't come up with anything new. Today Satan is again trying to eliminate the deliverers God is sending to us in our generation. Again his target is the young. For more than forty years now in America there has been a licensed assault against the most vulnerable of all—babies developing in the womb. It seems in our day that Satan's fear and intensity have escalated to unprecedented levels even for him. He must be really intimidated by God's plans for this generation if he cannot even wait until they are born to eliminate them.

Never has a generation been so assaulted and abused both inside and out of the womb. These are potential leaders, deliverers, and champions. We must recognize and respond to this satanic assault with an even greater intensity and devotion—we must pray for this chosen generation. We are in a battle for the destiny of a generation, and as a consequence, we are in a battle for the future they will define. Our enemy is great, but our God is greater. Our enemy is mighty, but our God is almighty. Our enemy is wily, but our God has all wisdom.

Our children and grandchildren were not born to become the latest casualties in Satan's assault on our youth, but rather the newest conquerors. We are supposed to win this spiritual battle, and we will as we understand the overcoming dominion of Spirit-enabled prayer!

We read in 2 Corinthians 10:3–5, "For though we live in the world, we do not wage war as the world does. The weapons we fight with are not the weapons of the world. On the contrary, they have divine power to demolish strongholds. We demolish arguments and every pretension that sets itself up against the knowledge of God, and we take captive every thought to make it obedient to Christ."

And Romans 8:31 says, "What then shall we say to these things? If God is for us, who can be against us?" (MEV).

A few verses later Scripture tells us, "Who shall separate us from the love of Christ? Shall tribulation, or distress, or persecution, or famine, or nakedness, or peril, or sword?…No, in all these things we are more than conquerors through Him who loved us. For I am persuaded that neither death nor life, neither angels nor principalities nor powers, neither things present nor things to come, neither height nor depth, nor any other created thing, shall be able to separate us from the love of God, which is in Christ Jesus our Lord" (Rom. 8:35, 37–39, MEV).

God is bigger than our obstacle, and through Christ we can triumph over the enemy. Our inheritance as children of God is victory.

WHAT'S IN A NAME?

Satan likes to insist that intelligence operates only in the absence of the knowledge of the one true God. How faulty, narrow, and shallow. Today, everywhere we cast our gaze in education and culture, we see intellectual development without an understanding of destiny. As the late pastor Myles Munroe stated, "When purpose is not known, abuse is inevitable."[1]

In his assault on the young Israelites in Babylon, one of Satan's first targets was their identity. In short order, their names were changed. Instead of names that spoke of their Hebrew heritage and purpose in God, they were given new Babylonian counterfeits. Daniel, Hananiah, Mishael, and Azariah became Belteshazzar, Shadrach, Meshach, and Abednego (Dan. 1:6–7).

Why is this so important? Because once we are disconnected from God's design for our life and His partnership in the fulfillment of His purpose for us, we can much more easily be influenced to pursue a substitute destiny.

I'm convinced from Scripture and life that we will never truly know who we are until we come to know Jesus Christ personally. While you were still in your mother's womb, God began to lovingly and uniquely author your life's plan. The psalmist wrote, "For you created my inmost being; you knit me together in my mother's womb. I praise you because I am fearfully and wonderfully made; your works are wonderful, I know that full well...Your eyes saw my unformed body; all the days ordained for me were written in your book before one of them came to be" (Ps. 139:13–14, 16). However, the ability to know and live out this plan is completely dependent on personally knowing Christ. Living life at the highest level is the result of God's intention joined with our decision to follow Him.

The name Daniel in Hebrew carries the meaning "God is my judge." Every time Daniel heard his name, he was reminded prophetically that the great Jehovah God was the one he answered to. But what does Babylon name him? Belteshazzar, meaning "Baal protects my life." Baal was a Babylonian idol so vile that even innocent children were burned as sacrifices in the twisted worship of this demonic god.[2] Jeremiah 19:5 says, "They have built the high places of Baal to burn their children in the fire as offerings to Baal—something I did not command or mention, nor did it enter my mind." Again we see the blatant attack against children. This thread of Satan attacking children, babies in particular, runs throughout the history of his evil strategy against the human race.

Hananiah's Hebrew name is translated "God has favored" or "Jehovah is gracious." The Babylonians changed his name to Shadrach, meaning, "I am at the command of the moon god." Talk about identity theft!

Mishael's name made it clear that God was his source; it is translated "who is like God." Every time his name was spoken he was reminded that there is no God like Jehovah! But in an attempt to indoctrinate him, Mishael was renamed Meshach. In a mockery of his God and his identity, the new name means "who is like Ahku," which was yet another demonic god.

Azariah's name change also pointed to the Babylonians' demonically inspired plan to alter the Israelites' identity. Azariah was a promising young man whose Hebrew name prophetically means "Jehovah is my help." His new name, Abednego, means "the servant of Nago [or Nebo]," which was another demonic idol.

The strategy here was blatant: steal their God-given identity and hijack their future.

I believe the enemy is doing the same thing to our children today. As I read about Daniel's journey in exile, I am amazed at the unmistakable similarities between his education in Babylon and the realities faced by this current generation in our secular school systems. Let me be quick to say that the goal of this book is not to launch a diatribe against all public education. Within the public school system are many teachers and administrators who are dedicated Christians. Not only do I recognize and support the remarkable ministry of these Christ followers in a sometimes restrictive system, I also try to be the best friend possible to our local schools.

I have many personal Christian friends and church members who serve our communities with excellence as teachers, administrators, coaches, and school faculty members. It is always easier to just stand by and curse the darkness than to get involved and make a positive difference. Our church supports our public schools with many prayer initiatives. Our parents are involved in PTA and PTO groups, and our members volunteer in the classrooms. We have placed food baskets in the teachers' lounges, and we have hosted several Educator Appreciation Days. We have given backpacks and school supplies to needy children at the start of the school year, and we help to provide food for at-risk children throughout the year. We are involved, and we care.

I am in no way trying to bash public schools. My concern is the deterioration of the overall spiritual and moral climate in our public school systems. Much of this, I know, is due to the dysfunction and breakdown of families and homes. Our schools are inundated and often overwhelmed as they attempt to educate children who bring with them to school each day the emotional and physical baggage of their desperate living conditions.

But rather than letting students begin their day with a prayer and a scripture that could give them hope, administrators are refusing to give God a permission slip to access school campuses. By the intent of the curriculum writers and those at the highest levels of education decision making, our schools are increasingly becoming "God-free zones." We no longer allow sodas, snacks, or a Savior. You can have juice, but not Jesus.

The biblical principles and moral foundations that once allowed our educational system to be a model for the world have been sidelined. Through legislation and judicial intimidation, the uplifting and enabling influence of God and His Word have now almost been removed from our children's educational experience.

So what are we going to do? How important are our children and grandchildren to us? Do we just take this lying down? *No!* We respond to this kneeling down! We must learn how to pray aggressively.

We are living in what the Bible defines as perilous times (2 Tim. 3:1, kjv). But that same powerful, inerrant, and proven Bible tells us that God has a plan for our children and students to overcome and be successful even in these times. Jesus said, "In this world you will have trouble. But take heart! I have overcome the world" (John 16:33). So come on! Let's accept the challenge—and let's get ready to rumble! This last round belongs to the people of God—and we're going to win!

There is so much to learn from and be encouraged by in the triumphant procession of Daniel's life. Daniel not only survived the attempts to rob his identity and misdirect his talents and gifts, but he also thrived in Babylon. Daniel was an overcomer who became one of the greatest influences in all recorded history. You may be wondering, "How?" Let me tell you simply: it was the power of prayer!

But it wasn't just any kind of prayer that protected Daniel from the influence of the ungodly culture that surrounded him. I refuse to waste your time by teaching you how to pray that your children will simply survive. I want to show you how to pray that they will become everything that God has designed them to be—godly, strong, smart, confident young leaders and influencers.

AGENTS OF CHANGE

God's will for your students is that they, like Daniel, live their lives at God's highest intent. When they do, they will not be changed by this culture but, rather, they will be the change agents. Like Daniel and his friends, they will be the influencers and not the influenced.

As I share the five principles of what I have come to call the Daniel Prayer, you may be forced to re-evaluate your understanding of what prayer encompasses and your role in its function here on earth. That's OK. It is my prayer that the truths that inspire this prayer will be imbedded in your heart and soul. Simply put, I want these principles to make their way deep into your heart, not merely into your mind.

I believe Daniel's story embodies what we want for our children, grandchildren, and students. He was only a teenager when he was captured and marched hundreds of miles to Babylon. His education in Babylon challenged everything he had been taught about God, but Daniel kept his faith as he excelled in his studies. In fact, Daniel did not just keep his faith in God; it actually grew stronger.

The current statistics concerning children raised in Christian homes stand in stark contrast to Daniel's story. According to the Barna Group, only about 30 percent of young people who grow up with a Christian background remain faithful to church and faith as they transition from their teen years to their twenties.[3] Something happens to these young people during their educational experience that is frankly disappointing. It's bad for our children, and it's bad for our future. We must find an answer—not an alibi. We are called to raise Daniels, not statistics.

Daniel was taken as a captive to a foreign land. He was of the wrong ethnic group, the wrong faith, and the wrong status. He was basically a slave—the spoils of war. Yet he proved his faith and character and, against every barrier, rose to the highest levels of government. And it all began while he was in school.

Daniel remained successful and godly during the reigns of more than half a dozen kings and three major dynasties—the Babylonians, the Medes, and the Persians. To fully appreciate the significance of that, you must realize that during that time, when a new king ascended the throne, he typically executed all the previous kingdom's officials. And if they weren't executed, they were exiled to prison and irrelevance.

But not Daniel! He influenced Babylon from the time he was a teenager until he was an old man in his eighties.

What a template for a life of overcoming faith and influence for God. My friend, this is God's design for your children. Daniel walked out this unparalleled legacy through the power of his prayer life. The Bible tells us that "three times a day he got down on his knees and prayed, giving thanks to his God," even when the king demanded that no one pray to anyone except him (Dan. 6:10). Prayer was Daniel's secret weapon, and I'm going to teach you how to pray in a way that will bring the same results for your family that Daniel experienced in his life. As we walk through this process, I will share the challenges and the testimonies—the answers to prayer—from my wonderful church family and friends.

Your prayers have an immeasurable impact on the lives of your children. They go before your children and clear the way for them to possess God's plan for their lives. They carry into the future and await God's perfect timing to be answered and fulfilled. Let me share with you one prayer victory that will illustrate what I've just said.

The young couple stood before the church to have their newborn son dedicated to God. The mother was overwhelmed with gratitude. God had not only given her a new son; He had given her a new husband. In answer to many prayers, her husband had recently come to know Christ as his Savior. As this child was being dedicated, they finally stood as a family that was one in Christ.

As the pastor prayed over the baby boy, the mother heard him make an unusual request. Very specifically, he prayed, "And, Lord, keep him safe from the wheels of a car."

Fast-forward more than thirty years. That simple prayer had almost been forgotten. Almost.

The day had started out well. The baby boy was now a young husband and father himself. He was on the way to his office, stopped at a traffic light. When the light turned green, he was the first car to move into the intersection. What he did not see was the car approaching the intersection from his left. Traveling over seventy miles per hour, the car blasted right through the red traffic light.

The young man never knew what hit him. His little Honda Civic crumpled on impact, and the force knocked his car into a ditch across four lanes of traffic. It was a direct hit on the driver's side, a common point of death and maiming in automobile accidents.

The driver of the other car actually struck one more vehicle before he finally stopped. The first ambulance to arrive on this scene did not even stop at the young father's car. They would later explain that because of past experience with these kinds of accidents, they went to the second car assuming the young father was already dead. They figured the next ambulance that arrived could take care of his body.

But God...

Someone had prayed, "Lord, keep him safe from the wheels of a car," and on that day, God did just that! That thirty-year-old prayer had no shelf life and was infused with a power greater than death.

I know that God answers prayers for children—because that baby boy was me! I know I am an answer to prayer... and so shall our children be!

Our church is, with excitement, learning the impact and

reward of biblical, focused, prevailing prayer, and we are also realizing that this kind of intercession is not optional or ritualistic. It is "boots-on-the-ground" spiritual conflict and engagement. Ephesians 6:10 says, "Finally, be strong in the Lord and in his mighty power." Our real battle is not with human personalities but with unseen spiritual principalities. We are equipped, empowered, and destined to win. But we must engage the enemy and exert the spiritual weapons God has given us.

Now that we see *why* we must pray, let's make sure we know *how* we should pray for our greatest treasures—our children and grandchildren, our families, our Daniels.

Chapter 2

BRINGING HEAVEN TO EARTH

Lord, teach us to pray.

—Luke 11:1, mev

T HERE IS A cry that resonates from deep within the spirit of everyone who begins to realize the power and possibilities of biblical prayer. It is the same cry that rose from Jesus's disciples when they began to connect Jesus's prayer life with the power and authority of His public life and ministry. That cry is, "Lord, teach us how to pray."

As Jesus began to respond to their hunger to learn how to pray, He taught the disciples principles, not just a formula to be memorized and mindlessly repeated. He taught them a pattern of prayer, an outline to guide them as they grew in their own personal prayer lifestyle. The "prayer starter" He taught them would emphasize the importance of worshipfully acknowledging God as their source, asking God to meet their needs, forgiving others and themselves, and asking for strength to overcome temptation as they represented Christ in their daily lives.

But before the disciples were to pray for any of those things, the very first request they were to make was this: "*Your* kingdom come; *Your* will be done on earth, as it is in heaven" (Matt. 6:10, mev, emphasis added). That's right. With those words, Jesus is showing us that prayer is the vehicle that brings God's will to earth. This is critical for us to understand. If we expect to truly learn how to pray, it all begins right here.

The kind of prayer that will pave the way for our beloved children to live overcoming, Christ-honoring lives will not be characterized by nebulous ambiguity or faithless fatalism. Biblical, Christ-centered prayer is not just begging for somebody, somewhere to please do something about a problem. It is not just a way we can anesthetize ourselves as we endure the injustices and onslaughts of a culture radically out of step with God's will.

God wants us to learn how to pray in a way that releases His kingdom—His will—here and now in our lives. He wants our prayers to become the doors that open this world to God's mercy, grace, love, and divine order. It is God's will that every one of your family members become strong followers of Christ, that they live lives of righteousness, significance, and loving service to God and man. It is His will that they completely fulfill every purpose He has designed for them. Our prayers must not settle for anything less.

We must become proactive and bold in prayer. Whatever our basic personalities may be, we must recognize what is at stake and throw off every limiting layer life has placed on us. This is not the time to be passive and of fragile faith as we pray. This is the time to go to spiritual war. A student, a child, a destiny hangs in the balance.

You may look at the ungodliness in the culture and the hostility toward God in our schools and think, "What can I do?" You can do a lot. You can be the difference maker. There is great hope for this generation, and right now I sense that God is gathering His people to prepare and position them through prayer.

We are a grassroots army, recruited by the Spirit of God. Together we are releasing a prayer tsunami that has the potential to lift an entire generation of Daniels. Together we are going to rewrite history by pushing back our children's enemies so they cannot destroy the promise and purpose of God for their lives.

We are quite an army! To the untrained eye, our uniforms may not seem to indicate we are on the same team. Some of us go to prayer/war each morning still in pajamas, a robe, or a housecoat; others wear workout gear; and some have on business suits or work uniforms. We may not be as color coordinated as some teams or as flamboyant as World Wrestling Entertainment, but do not be fooled by what your eyes alone can see. Unity and uniformity are not the same thing. This army is connected by a deep unity in the Spirit and a passion for a generation. You should not underestimate the unseen armament of God that fits well upon our inner man.

Our armor is spiritual, as the apostle Paul explained:

> Finally, be strong in the Lord and in his mighty power. Put on the full armor of God, so that you can take your stand against the devil's schemes. For our struggle is not against flesh and blood, but against the rulers, against the authorities, against the powers of this dark world and against the spiritual forces of evil in the heavenly realms. Therefore put on the full armor of God, so that when the day of evil comes, you may be able to stand your ground, and after you have done everything, to stand. Stand firm then, with the belt of truth buckled around your waist, with the breastplate of righteousness in place, and with your feet fitted with the readiness

that comes from the gospel of peace. In addition to all this, take up the shield of faith, with which you can extinguish all the flaming arrows of the evil one. Take the helmet of salvation and the sword of the Spirit, which is the word of God.

And pray in the Spirit on all occasions with all kinds of prayers and requests. With this in mind, be alert and always keep on praying for all the Lord's people.

—EPHESIANS 6:10–18

My prayer is that you will begin to learn how to pray from the inside out. What we look like, how old we are, and how bad our past may be should not limit our prayer life. Some of God's greatest warriors were at times overlooked and underestimated. God had to remind the prophet Samuel not to look at David's outward appearance when it was time to anoint a new king to succeed Saul.

But the LORD said to Samuel, "Do not look on his appearance or on the height of his stature, because I have rejected him. For the LORD sees not as man sees. For man looks on the outward appearance, but the LORD looks on the heart."

—1 SAMUEL 16:7, MEV

I sense in my spirit as I write this that God is calling you to a new confidence in prayer. I can see someone who has been beaten down by life rising up to join this prayer army. I can see unknown faces on earth being seated at the front of the table in heaven, seated near Christ, honored eternally because their prayers shaped the destiny of a generation. You have been chosen by God to be a mighty warrior in prayer— even if you don't think you look like one!

I was reminded of a valuable truth a few years ago when I had the privilege of meeting one of my spiritual heroes. The story of his healing, salvation, and call to ministry had always been so inspiring to me. As a church planter myself, I was amazed and encouraged to read of his humble beginnings planting a church in a castoff military tent that ultimately grew into one of the largest congregations in the world. Reading his books challenged me to pray more and grow in faith. As you can imagine, after a while he grew to a giant's stature in my mind.

Then the big day came. I was attending a conference that featured my spiritual hero as its keynote speaker. I had been invited to a gathering following the service that included an opportunity to meet him personally. The service was fantastic, and I could hardly wait to meet him afterward. Finally, the moment arrived. There I was, standing right in front of my spiritual hero, and was I ever surprised!

Because he was a hero in my eyes, I guess I somehow thought he would measure up to Superman or Thor in appearance. But as we shook hands, I realized my hero was four inches shorter than me and quite ordinary in appearance. Just as I was thinking that his stature wasn't at all what I imagined, I heard that familiar still, small voice in my spirit as God spoke to me: "You should see what he looks like on the inside."

Our status in life has nothing to do with our stature in prayer. Your prayers are more powerful than you think. But I believe God wants to take you to a new level in prayer for the children and the students in your life. So for the remainder of this chapter we are going to look at what I call the ABCs of prayer so you can learn how to pray in a way that brings supernatural results. Are you ready to begin?

A IS FOR AUTHORITY

The first key in learning how to pray is understanding our authority. Jesus said in the Gospel of Matthew, "All authority in heaven and on earth has been given to me. Therefore go and make disciples of all nations, baptizing them in the name of the Father and of the Son and of the Holy Spirit" (Matt. 28:18–19). What Jesus was saying here is that there's a new sheriff in town, and you are the deputy authorized to represent Him!

Knowing your authority is the most important principle in effective prayer. You are God's chosen representative to exercise His authority in your circle of influence. As author Dutch Sheets wrote in his book *Authority in Prayer*, "Satan didn't gain any power at the fall and didn't lose any at the cross. His power or ability didn't change at either event; his authority, or the right to use that power, did."[1] You see, power and authority are not synonymous biblical terms. When it comes to spiritual warfare and prayer, authority will always have the preeminent position of effectiveness, even over power. Let me illustrate.

Let's imagine we are driving down a six-lane highway and approaching a busy intersection. For some reason, the traffic light that directs and controls the flow of the automobiles at this important junction has ceased to operate properly. As the repair crew fervently works to restore the function of this traffic light, a policeman is standing in the intersection and directing the traffic. This officer at best weighs two hundred pounds, yet when he raises his hand, cars, trucks, and motor-cycles weighing hundreds of pounds come to a stop. The officer is not more powerful than the automobiles, but he has the delegated authority to bring their power into submission.

Just like the officer in that intersection, we as born-again believers have been delegated the authority of Jesus Christ, who won the victory over Satan on the cross. That means we too have the authority to stop Satan's power, and we exercise that authority through prayer.

Jesus said all authority in heaven and on earth has been given to Him. The Greek word translated "authority" in this passage is *exousia*. Unfortunately, in the wonderful King James Version of the Bible, the words *exousia* and *dunamis* are often both translated as "power." These words are very much connected, but they are quite different. *Dunamis* means strength, force, or might, while *exousia* is the right to exercise that force.

As you can see in the example of the police officer, the right to exercise authority will always prevail over the power of your adversary. Let's look at the word *exousia* in Scripture to make sure we see this distinction.

> Yet to all who received Him, He gave the power [*exousia*] to become sons of God, to those who believed in His name.
>
> —JOHN 1:12, MEV

> Then Jesus came to them and said, "All authority [*exousia*] in heaven and on earth has been given to me."
>
> —MATTHEW 28:18

In the second example, Jesus was referring to the authority that followed His atoning death on the cross and His triumphant resurrection from the grave. Notice that Jesus did not say all "power" was now His. His power—God's power—had never been in question. What had been regained through Jesus's death and resurrection was the authority God had given Adam—the delegated authority that Adam forfeited when he sinned in the Garden of Eden.

Neither God's authority in heaven nor His power were ever at risk. When Adam rebelled against God's word in the garden, he not only lost his delegated earthly authority, but Satan was then free to usurp Adam's position and become the de facto spiritual authority on earth. But Jesus's total victory on the cross stripped Satan of this stolen authority.

Remember, however, that Satan was not emptied of his power. This is why we must understand and enforce our authority as believers when we pray. As Dutch Sheets said, "Where God and Satan are concerned, the issue has never been power…it is always and only a question of authority."[2]

While reading the account of Jesus's baptism in Mark's Gospel one day, I discovered something interesting concerning Jesus, Satan, and the victorious restoration of God's authority on earth. Mark wrote:

> At that time Jesus came from Nazareth in Galilee and was baptized by John in the Jordan. Just as Jesus was coming up out of the water, he saw heaven being torn open and the Spirit descending on him like a dove.
>
> —MARK 1:9–10

The "heaven" mentioned in verse 10 (translated "the heavens" in the KJV) is not the dwelling place of God. It is referring to the atmosphere, or the region between earth and heaven. This is where the spiritual entities that affect the earth are located, and this is where spiritual warfare is engaged.

Mark tells us that as Jesus was coming out of the water, He saw the heavens being "torn open." This was not a pleasant parting, but rather a cleaving asunder, or a rending. It was literally a forceful tearing open. What was happening? The next sentence helps us understand.

As Jesus rose from the Jordan River, the Holy Spirit descended to anoint Him in a preview of what would follow for the church. Satan's evil spiritual atmosphere of authority had been confronted. Satan did not welcome this fresh invasion of the Holy Spirit, but he could not stop it! The Spirit of God ripped a hole in Satan's tapestry of deadly authority, and when Jesus died and rose again the restoration of authority became complete.

By the way, the term translated "torn open" in Mark 1:10, the Greek word *schizō*, is also used in Matthew 27:51, where we read that the veil in the temple hiding the holy of holies was "torn in two from top to bottom" at Jesus's victorious sacrifice on the cross. Again we see God establishing a new order. Satan was defeated, and every believer was now able to access the presence of God. In much the same way, God will tear through every obstacle to see that your prayers will be answered.

In the Old Testament, Moses's rod is a symbol of the believer's delegated authority in prayer. When Moses extended his rod of authority at God's command, plagues were released and the Red Sea parted. But before this could happen, Moses had to submit to God's will and obey Him.

Moses's miraculous rod of authority had once just been an ordinary shepherd's staff. Yet when Moses took his hands off his life and his staff, and threw it down at God's command, everything changed. (See Exodus 4:3.)

At the time Moses chose to follow God, he was afraid to go back to Egypt and face Pharaoh and his past. He was insecure about his leadership skills and his ability to speak. But finally he learned what you and I must learn about God's delegated authority. Our authority doesn't come from who we are or what we have or haven't done. It comes from Jesus's total victory on the cross and our complete surrender to Him. We do not pray in our own power or ability; it's praying in the authority we have through Christ that releases God's power.

But *having* authority isn't the same as using it. Just as Moses had to learn how this God-given authority operated through his life, so must we.

In Exodus 14 we find Moses still struggling to understand how God's authority worked in his life. The Israelites had just been miraculously liberated from their long Egyptian bondage, but Pharaoh had second thoughts. The Egyptian army was furiously pursuing the Israelites, and God's people found themselves trapped between the rapidly advancing war machine and the Red Sea. The people—and Moses—seemed to have suddenly developed a severe case of spiritual amnesia, forgetting the miracles and stunning displays of power God had just demonstrated when He freed them from Egypt.

Now, this is the critical moment. Notice what God said to Moses: "Why are you crying out to me? Tell the Israelites to move on. *Raise your staff* and stretch out your hand over the sea to divide the water so that the Israelites can go through the sea on dry ground" (Exod. 14:15–16, emphasis added). God told Moses to stop crying and use his authority. He basically said, "Raise your staff—your authority—and *you* do something!"

What does that look like in our lives? Praying with authority is not begging or pleading with God; it is declaring and decreeing what God has already established in His Word. His Word is His will, so stand up against your "Red Sea" and command it to line up with God's will.

A decree is a royal edict or command. The ruling sovereign makes a decree, and it becomes the law of the land. Whenever the decree is read or repeated, it carries the full weight or authority of its author. Its impact is not measured by the one who publishes it, but always and only by the ruler who authored it. When you proclaim a decree, it is as if the author of the decree himself is speaking. (See Daniel 6:26.)

In the same way, to "declare" is to make known, tell, publish, or proclaim something. The connotation is that of a messenger repeating the edict of his superior. John wrote, "This is the message we have heard from him and declare to you; God is light; in him there is no darkness at all" (1 John 1:5). John was declaring something he had been told.

We can do the same. In fact, that is how we exercise our authority in Christ. We can take our prayers to another level by understanding our authority. It doesn't come from us; it comes from the King of all kings.

At some point Moses had to realize, "It's not about you, Moses. Just raise the rod." It's not about you or me either—what we think we can or cannot do. We just need to pray. When you pray for your child or your student with the authority you have in Christ, victory is secure.

All authority on earth was placed securely in Jesus's hands when He defeated death, hell, and the grave. The Scriptures say, "And having disarmed the powers and authorities, he made a public spectacle of them, triumphing over them by the cross" (Col. 2:15). With salvation won on the cross and forever secured by the Resurrection, the authority of Christ has been delegated to the church.

Through Christ, your prayer is the authorized vehicle to release God's power into every situation your Daniels will encounter. It's not your power or perceived weakness against Satan and his kingdom—it's the authority of Christ, backed up by all the power of heaven, that is released as you pray.

Jesus said, "I have given you authority [*exousia*] to trample on snakes and scorpions and to overcome *all* the power [*dunamis*] of the enemy; nothing will harm you" (Luke 10:19, emphasis added). That's the confidence you should have as you pray, deputy! You're walking in the authority you've been given by Christ, and *nothing* is more powerful than He is—not our secular culture or an educational system that wants to kick God off campus.

But we're just getting started. Let's build on this understanding of authority in prayer by discovering the *B* in our ABCs of prayer: establishing boundary lines.

B IS FOR BOUNDARY LINES

As we continue to learn how to pray for our children, we must take a fresh look at a familiar "prayer word." One of the terms often used in discussing prayer is *intercession*. There are several words used in the New Testament to describe prayer and its function, and each one gives us a different view of what prayer includes. So just what can we learn from the term *intercession*?

Accurately and most commonly we define intercession as making an appeal—to meet with, go on behalf of someone or something, and present his need to the one capable of assisting. In prayer, we present the needs of those around us to our great God, who is able to meet the need out of His unlimited grace and provision. What a privilege to connect heaven and earth in believing prayer. Intercessors—those who are willing to pray on behalf of others—are incredible friends and gifts in life.

But what does intercession have to do with establishing boundary lines? And what kind of boundary lines are we talking about? Boundaries that define our limitations, or a different kind of boundary?

The Hebrew counterpart of the New Testament term translated "to intercede" is *pagha*. This word occurs in the Old Testament forty-six times in the King James Version. In Joshua 19, we find *pagha* used five times. On the surface, this chapter does not seem to be exciting reading (not to diminish the value of every word of Scripture, of course; I know how much you enjoy reading Leviticus!). But let's take a second look here, because this chapter has much to teach us about intercession.

Though the word *pagha* can be translated "make intercession" (as well as to "make entreaty" or even to "make attack"), in Joshua 19 it is translated "reaches to" or "extends to," as the chapter explains where the boundary lines of the Israelites' inheritance were established. Those boundary lines reflected what God wanted for His children, but the people of Israel still had to take the territory. God mapped out His will, but the Israelites had to go to war to see His will become a reality.

I believe true intercession is going to war in prayer so that every plan and purpose that God has designed for our children will be realized—that they will grow in their faith and personal relationship with Christ until they are in full possession of God's highest intent for their lives. The boundary lines established as we intercede for our children are not narrow, limiting, legalistic restraints. Rather, as we pray bold, determined, warfare prayers, our children are released to become everything they dare to ask or imagine—and more.

Our intercession can define the destiny—the inheritance—of a generation. That is the purpose for prayer that we read about in the following verses:

> Remember the former things of old, for I am God, and there is no other; I am God, and there is no one like Me, declaring the end from the beginning, and from ancient times the things that are not yet done, saying, "My counsel shall stand, and I will do all My good pleasure," calling a ravenous bird from the east, the man who executes My counsel from a far country. Indeed, I have spoken it; I will also bring it to pass. I have purposed it; I will also do it.
> —ISAIAH 46:9–11, MEV

But this is what the LORD says: "Yes, captives will be taken from warriors, and plunder retrieved from the fierce; I will contend with those who contend with you, and your children I will save."

—ISAIAH 49:25

All your children will be taught by the LORD, and great will be their peace. In righteousness you will be established: Tyranny will be far from you; you will have nothing to fear. Terror will be far removed; it will not come near you. If anyone does attack you, it will not be my doing; whoever attacks you will surrender to you.

—ISAIAH 54:13–15

"No weapon forged against you will prevail, and you will refute every tongue that accuses you. This is the heritage of the servants of the LORD, and this is their vindication from me," declares the LORD.

—ISAIAH 54:17

So is my word that goes out from my mouth: It will not return to me empty, but will accomplish what I desire and achieve the purpose for which I sent it.

—ISAIAH 55:11

As you pray for your children, grandchildren, or any student, think of Joshua leading the nation of Israel as it finally possessed its promised inheritance in Canaan. The army would have to go in to dislodge the enemies that dwelt in the strongholds of the land of God's promise. But before the Israelites could conquer the land, a mental transformation had to take place.

All they had known year after year was promises that had not come to pass and paths that seemed to lead nowhere as they wandered through the wilderness for forty years. Now that it was time to possess their inheritance, these former slaves and current nomads had to be transformed into well-oiled fighting machines because they would face unparalleled opposition.

To take the territory God mapped out for them, the Israelites would need a new level of trust in God. For the sake of their children and families, they could no longer settle for the status quo. This is why repeatedly in the Book of Joshua we see God telling the people to be strong and courageous:

- "Be strong and courageous, because you will lead these people to inherit the land I swore to their ancestors to give them" (Josh. 1:6).

- "Be strong and very courageous" (Josh. 1:7, MEV).

- "Have not I commanded you? Be strong and courageous. Do not be afraid or dismayed, for the LORD your God is with you wherever you go" (Josh. 1:9, MEV).

- "Only be strong and courageous!" (Josh. 1:18).

You are authorized by Jesus's total victory on the cross to release God's will on earth. You are in this army of prayer, and what you do in intercession is invaluable and unassailable by the forces of hell. You must rout the satanic minions and demonic strongholds that would seek to prevent your children from possessing the destiny God has designed for them. But like the Israelites, you must first make the transition in your mind and spirit from helpless observer to authorized, empowered intercessor, boldly and courageously winning the prayer battle as you advance to possess every square inch of your family's spiritual inheritance.

If the Israelites could make this mental shift and conquer all the nations that opposed them, consider this: you're being led on this holy campaign by one greater than Joshua. Hebrews 7:25 informs us that Jesus Christ, the reigning King of the universe and Captain of the hosts of heaven, "always lives to intercede for" His people! You are being led by the greatest intercessor and have been delegated His authority! In Jesus's name, you are authorized to rebuke Satan from your children's lives and destiny so they can occupy their God-given inheritance.

Your determination to wholeheartedly intercede for your children each day has an incalculable effect on their future. Let me illustrate. David's journey from shepherd to king of Israel is an encouraging, faith-building account. As you know, he was first recognized as king only over the house of Judah before all of Israel finally established him as king over the nation. (See 2 Samuel 2:1–4.) What I want you to notice is the radically different experiences he had in the two cities in which he reigned.

When he was initially accepted by the tribe of Judah, he was anointed as king and lived in the area of Hebron. There David and his family were welcomed and lived in peace, and the next season of his promised reign as king was established. After David spent seven successful years in Hebron, the elders of Israel finally decided to travel to Hebron and anoint him king over all of Israel.

Hebron was the springboard to David's destiny as king over God's people. It was a warm, safe, welcoming place where David was able to flourish in God's purpose for his life. But when David left Hebron to be enthroned in the capitol city, the holy city of Jerusalem, everything changed. David could not even enter the city because it was occupied by the fierce and mocking Jebusites. (See 2 Samuel 5:1–10.) David entered Hebron at the head of the parade, but he would have to march against Jerusalem at the head of an army. Why was David's experience in these two cities so different?

It has to do with who went before him to establish the boundary lines of Israel's inheritance. Do you remember that out of all the Hebrew adults who left Egypt for the Promised Land, only Joshua and Caleb were able to actually enter in? Everyone else not only forfeited their own inheritance but that of their children as well by their constant doubting, disobedience, and murmuring. How did Joshua and Caleb rise above the toxic atmosphere in a nation that would rather complain than conquer? Numbers 14:24 gives us the answer: "But because my servant Caleb has a different spirit and follows me wholeheartedly, I will bring him into the land he went to, and his descendants will inherit it." Caleb followed God wholeheartedly. Never forget: the boundaries of your heart will define the boundaries of your life!

Caleb had a "different spirit," a phrase that means a "next spirit." It refers to someone who has faith to reach for what God has next, someone who refuses to settle for less for himself or his family. So what did Mr. "Different Spirit" do when he arrived in the Promised Land? Joshua 14 gives us this fascinating account:

> "I was forty years old when Moses the servant of the
> LORD sent me from Kadesh Barnea to explore the

land. And I brought him back a report according to my convictions, but my fellow Israelites who went up with me made the hearts of the people melt in fear. I, however, followed the LORD my God wholeheartedly. So on that day Moses swore to me, 'The land on which your feet have walked will be your inheritance and that of your children forever, because you have followed the LORD my God wholeheartedly.'

"Now then, just as the LORD promised, he has kept me alive for forty-five years since the time he said this to Moses, while Israel moved about in the wilderness. So here I am today, eighty-five years old! I am still as strong today as the day Moses sent me out; I'm just as vigorous to go out to battle now as I was then. Now give me this hill country that the LORD promised me that day. You yourself heard then that the Anakites were there and their cities were large and fortified, but, the LORD helping me, I will drive them out just as he said."

Then Joshua blessed Caleb son of Jephunneh and gave him Hebron as his inheritance. So Hebron has belonged to Caleb son of Jephunneh the Kenizzite ever since, because he followed the LORD, the God of Israel, wholeheartedly. (Hebron used to be called Kiriath Arba after Arba, who was the greatest man among the Anakites.)

Then the land had rest from war.

—JOSHUA 14:7–15

Did you catch that? Caleb was known as a man who spent his life following God wholeheartedly; reaching for what was next; interceding, establishing, and occupying boundary lines. And where did Caleb defeat Israel's enemies and establish the kingdom's reach? Hebron. And where was David, centuries later, first recognized as king? Hebron. David did not have to fight for his inheritance in Hebron because Caleb had already done so. God wants to use you to effect this very same victory for those who will come after you.

The contrast between Hebron and Jerusalem is striking. Jerusalem was just as much a part of God's purpose for David as was Hebron. But that city was much more difficult for David to occupy. Why? It's because David couldn't occupy that city until he defeated the enemies his forefathers had refused to conquer.

The Jebusites were stubborn and unwilling to leave their territory when David's ancestors engaged them in battle. These earlier Israelites could have defeated them and paved the way for David. They had the same God Caleb did but not the same heart. They had the same promises but not the same persistence.

We cannot afford to make halfhearted attempts to establish the boundary lines of inheritance for future generations. Like Caleb, we must follow God wholeheartedly and leave our children a legacy of victory.

Now that we've covered the *A* of authority and the *B* of boundary lines, it's time to move to the C in the ABCs of prayer.

C IS FOR CONTRACTUAL PRAYER

Just what is contractual prayer? Remember that God has inseparably linked His will taking place on earth to the prayers of His people. In his prayer guide *Devotional Living*, author Desmond T. Evans states that contractual prayer is represented by the Greek word *deesis*, which is most often translated "supplication."[3] Evans goes on to say supplication, or contractual prayer, is "bringing into being the will of God—praying that which was ordained before the foundations of the world will be actualized in time. It is a plea for the evidence of divine order."[4]

Contractual prayer is literally God's will and a Christian's prayer coming into agreement to release God's purpose and order in the here and now. It is a prayer that opens the door for what God has planned to be experienced here on earth. Could it be that we keep waiting on God to "do something" when He just may be waiting on us to do something—pray. God's purposes and plans were decided upon before the beginning of time. But to experience the actuality of God's plan in time, we must partner with God in prayer.

In Hebrews 5:7 we find this word *deesis*, or supplication, used to describe Jesus's prayer life: "In the days of His flesh, Jesus offered up prayers and supplications with loud cries and tears to Him who was able to save Him from death. He was heard because of His godly fear" (Heb. 5:7, MEV). Most Bible teachers agree that this verse refers to the moment when Jesus was praying in the Garden of Gethsemane. His "reverent submission" to the Father was stated in His final surrender to the cross: "Thy will be done" (Matt. 26:42, KJV). I don't want you to miss this perfect example of supplication, or contractual prayer.

In Revelation 13:8, we are told that Jesus was "the Lamb slain from the foundation of the world" (KJV). And yet, what God had ordained in eternity past awaited an earthly respondent to release His will to be done. The plan of God and the hope of salvation for all mankind hung in the balance as Jesus's humanity wrestled in contractual prayer to agree with God's will. His prayer discerned and connected with God's will, and this enabled Jesus to actually go and do God's will. Without an earthly countersign to heaven's plan, mankind will never experience all that God has designed. Answered prayer will always have a heaven side and an earth side.

I know this awareness of man's role in prayer may make some uneasy. Many would prefer to think that whatever God wills is automatically done. Certainly, God can do anything He chooses—and that is exactly what we must understand. God does not have to partner with redeemed men and women to fulfill His purposes, but He has chosen to do so. It's not that He cannot but rather that He will not.

Some seem to struggle with man's partnership with God in prayer simply because they shy away from accepting their responsibility. Yet we read in James 4:2, "You do not have because you do not ask God." I would much rather believe that we can know God's will and partner with Him in prayer concerning our children than just live my life hoping and wishing all goes well. The times demand that we throw off the martyr complex and leave behind the victim mentality. Your children are too important for religious-sounding excuses and thinly veiled fatalism. You have access to the very throne of God in Jesus's name, and when you ask according to His will, He hears you and answers you. First John 5:14–15 says, "This is the confidence we have in approaching God: that if we ask anything according to his will, he hears us. And if we know that he hears us—whatever we ask—we know that we have what we asked of him."

Contractual prayer is the overflow of a fresh and growing personal relationship with Christ. It is important to note that in this prayer partnership, we are not giving God the plan or directions; He is conveying His will to us. We simply acknowledge God's purpose and then faithfully stand in prayer to release the reign of His kingdom here and now on earth. How do we know His will? That comes through relationship.

As our relationship with Christ matures and develops, so does our understanding of God and His will. The more time we devote to reading our Bibles, the clearer God's will becomes to us. Why? Because His Word *is* His will. Studying God's Word regularly will cause His voice to become clearer and our faith to grow much stronger. In the same way, as our prayer time becomes more consistent, it will become easier for us to recognize God's voice. There's no formula for growing closer to God; it's just the result of time spent in His presence.

When my wife calls me, I recognize her voice immediately. There's no need for her to identify herself. Our communication is easy and natural because I've spent time with her, listening to her.

That's exactly how we come to pray with authority and confidence. When we know God's Word and His voice through our relationship with Him, we are able to pray His will. God's voice will always be in agreement with His Word, the Bible.

You can partner with God, and He will use your prayer to establish His will for your children. Let's take a fresh look at a familiar passage of Scripture in light of our understanding of contractual prayer.

> And I tell you that you are Peter, and on this rock I
> will build My church, and the gates of Hades shall
> not prevail against it. I will give you the keys of
> the kingdom of heaven, and whatever you bind on
> earth shall be bound in heaven, and whatever you
> loose on earth shall be loosed in heaven.
>
> —MATTHEW 16:18–19, MEV

What a powerfully encouraging statement concerning you and me, the church. Authority, keys, binding and loosing—God has expressed some pretty lofty confidence in you. You literally represent and distribute God's will and resources on earth! You have keys to open and close doors of great spiritual significance that impact earthly situations. Your prayers can bind, restrict, or tie up God's adversaries and bring freedom to those that life and Satan have put in chains.

To deepen our understanding of the power we have been given, I want to quote Jack Hayford's careful paraphrase of this same passage:

> Whatever you may at any time encounter (of hell's
> counsels which I'm declaring my Church shall pre-
> vail against), you will then face a decision as to
> whether you will or won't bind it. What transpired
> will be conditional upon your response. If you do
> personally and consciously involve yourself in the
> act of binding the issue on earth, you will discover
> that at that future moment when you do, that it
> has already been bound in heaven."[5]

Wow! Are you getting the message? What you pray matters. God has declared His will and provided His resources. Now He awaits your response.

I want to share one final perspective on this defining job description of the church found in Matthew 16:18–19. The most obvious definition of "bind" is to tie or wrap with rope. But there is another use of this word that sheds a bright spotlight on contractual prayer. *Bind* is also used in a legal, contractual sense, as in a binding agreement or to bind yourself with an oath.

With this legal definition in mind, "binding" can be understood as actually contracting with God. He has determined His will and in essence has signed His name to the contract. All that separates earth, your children, and your family from encountering all that God can do is your countersignature as you agree with Him in prayer. So let's do this! As Paul E. Billheimer is quoted as saying, "Satan does not care how many people read about prayer if only he can keep them from praying."[6]

We have learned why and how we should pray. Now in the next section we will explore what we should pray. We will get specific so we can clearly focus our prayers for our children, grandchildren, and students. As I stated earlier, it is very important to understand the powerful biblical principles of the Daniel Prayer for Parents. There is a major difference between just repeating a prayer formula and declaring a Spirit-enabled, faith-filled, prophetic prayer.

Using Daniel and his fellow young Jewish exiles' experience in Babylon, in the next section I will share with you five distinct prayer focuses for your children. Daniel chapter 1 will be the vein from which we mine these prayer principles. If you allow these truths to shape your daily prayer for your children,

I am confident they will be positioned to receive God's best as they head off to school and navigate through life.

Are you ready? Let's dig in and see what God has for us to discover. Your children will forever thank you for the life you are about to establish for them as you pray.

Part 2

PRAYING THE DANIEL PRAYER

Chapter 3

PRAYER PRINCIPLE #1:
HEALTH AND HEALING

*...young men who were healthy and handsome, intelligent
and well-educated, good prospects for leadership
positions in the government, perfect specimens!*

—DANIEL 1:4

A S THE VERSE at the beginning of this chapter attests,
Daniel and his friends were anything but average. We
will discuss their intellect and influence in later chapters, but
for now I want to focus on the first quality mentioned in this
verse. Daniel and his friends were in good health.

I don't know of any parent who wants his child to be sick,
and I have some really good news—God doesn't either. In
fact, I'm convinced that God is even more concerned for our
children's health than we are. God is not only able but also
willing to bring healing and health to our children. That is
why one of the most important prayers we can offer to God
each day is for our children's physical health.

Scripture clearly reveals God's power and desire to heal.
God said in the Book of Exodus:

> "If you diligently listen to the voice of the LORD your
> God, and do what is right in His sight, and give ear
> to His commandments, and keep all His statutes,
> I will not afflict you with any of the diseases with

> which I have afflicted the Egyptians. *For I am the
> LORD who heals you.*"
>
> —EXODUS 15:26, MEV, EMPHASIS ADDED

Early in Scripture, as God was revealing Himself to the children of Israel, we discover that His very nature is to heal. The word translated "heal" in Exodus 15:26 is the Hebrew term *rapha*. Strong's Concordance defines this word as to cure, heal, repair, mend, restore health. Clearly the central meaning is physical healing, but God does not stop there. He joins His very name to this healing word. He declares, "I am the LORD who heals you." He is saying, "I am *Yahweh-Rapha*." God reveals that His very name—His perfect, divine nature—is to heal.

God declares Himself to be the healer of our bodies throughout the Old and New Testaments. In Isaiah 53, the great prophetic chapter pointing to Christ's atoning death on the cross, we find a promise confirmed by both Jesus and the church.

> Surely he took up our pain and bore our suffering,
> yet we considered him punished by God, stricken by
> him, and afflicted. But he was pierced for our trans-
> gressions, he was crushed for our iniquities; the pun-
> ishment that brought us peace was on him, and by
> his wounds [also translated "stripes"] we are healed.
>
> —ISAIAH 53:4–5

Does this passage refer to spiritual, emotional, or physical healing? The answer is simply, *"Yes!"* This is not an either-or promise; it is all-inclusive. But we can be sure that this does, in fact, include physical healing when we fast-forward to Jesus's ministry in Matthew's Gospel:

> When the evening came, they brought to Him
> many who were possessed with demons. And He
> cast out the spirits with His word, and healed all
> who were sick, to fulfill what was spoken by Isaiah
> the prophet, "He Himself took our infirmities and
> bore our sicknesses."
> —MATTHEW 8:16–17, MEV

We find yet another reference to the promise and provision of healing prophesied in Isaiah 53 when we read Peter's first epistle: "'He himself bore our sins' in his body on the cross, so that we might die to sins and live for righteousness; 'by his wounds you have been healed'" (1 Pet. 2:24). As Peter writes under the direction of the Holy Spirit, we are given another perspective. From this vantage point, looking back on the finished work of Christ on the cross, our healing is seen as already done. We read that we "have been healed." The provision has been made. The price has been paid. Healing is yours, my friend, to humbly, thankfully, and with great confidence declare over your children as you pray for them daily.

It's one thing to have a promise of healing and another to experience the fulfillment of the promise. Let me encourage you here with an incredible story of God's healing a young man I know. He and his family attend Calvary, and he is a walking miracle, a constant reminder that God heals today. This is Conner's story, told by his very thankful mother, Marie.[1]

> During my pregnancy I suffered a violent attack,
> and as a result Conner was brought into this world
> eight weeks premature. When he was born, the
> doctors said he had no ability to breathe and had
> water on his brain because of the attack on me
> the day before. They rushed him out of the room

and brought him back in so I could say good-bye because he needed to be rushed to another hospital in Huntsville, Alabama. I was told he wouldn't survive through the night, so nine hours later I checked myself out of the hospital to go be with him.

When I arrived in Huntsville, Conner was on a breathing machine, and his head was swollen. My first response was to ask God why He gave me this child to just take him away. I asked Conner's grandfather to come pray over him, and every time he prayed with Conner, he seemed to improve. The last day he prayed with Conner, he asked me to leave so he could pray alone with him. To everyone's surprise, the next day Conner was taken off the breathing tube. He came home a week later. The doctors said he wouldn't survive, and to all their amazement Conner went home in a month. This was all God.

I never get tired of hearing that testimony. Conner has faced other health challenges in his young life, but his family has declared God's promise of healing over him, and he continues to defy the odds. Young Conner is truly a testament to God's power—and willingness—to heal. Though his mother is still contending for his health, God is moving mightily in that young man's life.

And while we're on the subject of healing, let's get something settled right here: God is not the author of sickness and death. He is the healer and giver of life. Sickness and disease can be clearly traced to the Fall, the original sin of Adam and Eve. Sickness was introduced to the human experience as a result of the curse of sin, and every human being on the planet is susceptible to its consequences.

The good news is that Jesus's death on the cross dealt with all the aftereffects of the fall of man. In other words, everything Adam's sin cost us was restored by Christ. For our sins, God made forgiveness available to all. In response to death, God provided eternal life. With regard to sickness, God has mercifully supplied healing.

The blood Jesus shed on the cross is all-sufficient. Wherever you or your family members are broken, Jesus is your healer. His redemption includes your whole person and your child's whole person—body, soul, and spirit. It's like the lyrics of Ricardo Sanchez's incredible song "The Power of the Cross." It says in essence that nothing is missing or broken—it is finished because Jesus's blood has spoken. Isn't that powerful?

GOD IS WILLING TO HEAL

John 1:14 tells us that when Jesus came to this earth to be our Savior, He was God's Word made flesh. In other words, He was God's perfect will walking around in human form. He revealed God and His will to us. Everything He said and did was a clear example of how God speaks, thinks, and acts. So how did Jesus respond to sickness and disease?

> Jesus went throughout all Galilee teaching in their synagogues, preaching the gospel of the kingdom, and healing all kinds of sickness and all sorts of diseases among the people. His fame went throughout all Syria. And they brought to Him all sick people who were taken with various diseases and tormented with pain, those who were possessed with

demons, those who had seizures, and those who had paralysis, and He healed them.

—MATTHEW 4:23–24, MEV

Jesus went throughout all the cities and villages, teaching in their synagogues, preaching the gospel of the kingdom, and healing every sickness and every disease among the people.

—MATTHEW 9:35, MEV

In the evening, when the sun had set, they brought to Him all who were sick and those who were possessed with demons. The whole city was gathered at the door, and He healed many who were sick with various diseases and cast out many demons. And He did not let the demons speak, because they knew Him.

—MARK 1:32–34, MEV

Now when the sun was setting, all those who had anyone sick with various diseases brought them to Him. And He laid His hands on every one of them and healed them.

—LUKE 4:40, MEV

With encounter after encounter, we see that Jesus healed "all" who were sick. It's very important for you to be certain that healing is not selective. You and your children are qualified to be healed because Jesus took stripes on His back so that you could be healed—and God desires to heal.

It is not our qualifications that matter the most; it is our justification. The fact that we have been redeemed by the Cross and forgiven of our sins positions us for every benefit of salvation. As you pray for health and healing, keep your eyes on God and His promises, not your worthiness or unworthiness. Our emotions and even our faith may rise and fall, but our God is sure and constant.

I love this exchange between Jesus and a leper in Mark chapter 1:

> A man with leprosy came to him and begged him on his knees, "If you are willing, you can make me clean." Jesus was indignant. He reached out his hand and touched the man. "I am willing," he said. "Be clean!" Immediately the leprosy left him and he was cleansed.
>
> —MARK 1:40–42

The focus of this passage is God's will concerning physical healing. This encounter is included in Matthew, Mark, and Luke, and it is the only time recorded in Jesus's earthly ministry when the subject of healing asks "if" Jesus was willing.

And how did Jesus respond? He said, "I am willing." Only once was Jesus asked, "Is healing Your will?" And His answer was clear and to the point: "I am willing."

As you are praying for your child to be healed, you must pray believing that, yes, it is God's will for your child to be healed. Once you have that settled in your mind and spirit, there is a powerful promise you must let sink deep in your heart. It is found in the First Epistle of John: "This is the confidence we have in approaching God: that if we ask anything according to his will, he hears us. And if we know that he hears us—whatever we ask—we know that we have what we asked of him" (1 John 5:14–15).

How great is that?

We have so much to be encouraged about as we see the heart of God concerning healing revealed through Jesus's ministry. But healing did not stop there. The Book of Acts, which is our record of the formation of the church, is replete with accounts of healing. The preaching of the gospel was inseparably linked with divine healing. God's power demonstrated through transformational salvation and healing was the one-two punch that propelled the gospel throughout the known world.

God clearly transferred the earthly healing ministry of Jesus to the church. Notice how the message of salvation and the ministry of healing marched across the miles and the decades as the church continued to grow:

> One day Peter and John were going up to the temple at the time of prayer—at three in the afternoon. Now a man who was lame from birth was being carried to the temple gate called Beautiful, where he was put every day to beg from those going into the temple courts. When he saw Peter and John about to enter, he asked them for money. Peter looked straight at him, as did John. Then Peter said, "Look at us!" So the man gave them his attention, expecting to get something from them.
>
> Then Peter said, "Silver or gold I do not have, but what I do have I give you. In the name of Jesus Christ of Nazareth, walk." Taking him by the right hand, he helped him up, and instantly the man's feet and ankles became strong. He jumped to his feet and began to walk. Then he went with them into the temple courts, walking and jumping, and praising God. When all the people saw him walking and praising God, they recognized him as the same man who used to sit begging at the temple gate called Beautiful, and they were filled

with wonder and amazement at what had happened to him.

—Acts 3:1–10

Believers were increasingly added to the Lord, crowds of both men and women, so that they even brought the sick out into the streets and placed them on beds and mats, that at least the shadow of Peter passing by might touch some of them. Crowds also came out of the cities surrounding Jerusalem, bringing the sick and those who were afflicted by evil spirits, and they were all healed.

—Acts 5:14–16, mev

Therefore those who were scattered went everywhere preaching the word. Philip went down to the city of Samaria and preached Christ to them. When the crowds heard Philip and saw the miracles which he did, they listened in unity to what he said. For unclean spirits, crying with a loud voice, came out of many who were possessed. And many who were paralyzed or lame were healed. So there was much joy in that city.

—Acts 8:4–8, mev

From city to city, hope and healing were spreading. And in Samaria, it was not an apostle but a deacon whom God was using. God's power and mercy to heal cannot be locked down to a time frame or a title. If you are willing to ask, God is willing to answer.

Never forget that healing not only alleviates our pain and suffering, but it also causes people to turn to Christ.

As Peter traveled about the country, he went to visit the Lord's people who lived in Lydda. There he found a man named Aeneas, who was paralyzed and had been bedridden for eight years. "Aeneas," Peter said to him, "Jesus Christ heals you. Get up and roll up your mat." Immediately Aeneas got up. *All those who lived in Lydda and Sharon saw him and turned to the Lord.*

In Joppa there was a disciple named Tabitha (in Greek her name is Dorcas); she was always doing good and helping the poor. About that time she became sick and died, and her body was washed and placed in an upstairs room. Lydda was near Joppa; so when the disciples heard that Peter was in Lydda, they sent two men to him and urged him, "Please come at once!"

Peter went with them, and when he arrived he was taken upstairs to the room. All the widows stood around him, crying and showing him the robes and other clothing that Dorcas had made while she was still with them.

Peter sent them all out of the room; then he got down on his knees and prayed. Turning toward the dead woman, he said, "Tabitha, get up." She opened her eyes, and seeing Peter she sat up. He took her by the hand and helped her to her feet. Then he called for the believers, especially the widows, and presented her to them alive. This became known all over Joppa, and *many people believed in the Lord*. Peter stayed in Joppa for some time with a tanner named Simon.

—ACTS 9:32–43, EMPHASIS ADDED

What might happen in your child's school as a result of your child being healed?

These tremendous accounts of divine healing continue throughout the Book of Acts. The trajectory was set, and

God has not changed His mind or diminished in His power to heal. In fact, as we read the Book of Acts and the epistles that follow, the ministry and availability of healing does not decrease; it increases.

The New Testament begins with God's power to heal primarily flowing through Jesus. As the church begins in Acts, this healing provision initially expands through the apostles. Then the circle widens again, and in Acts 8 Philip the deacon is used by God to release healing.

Now look with me in James chapter 5. At this point in Scripture we are near the end of the apostolic age, and rather than a cessation of divine healing, God promises healing to every local gathering of believers on the planet.

> Is anyone among you sick? Let them call the elders of the church to pray over them and anoint them with oil in the name of the Lord. And the prayer offered in faith will make the sick person well; the Lord will raise them up. If they have sinned, they will be forgiven. Therefore confess your sins to each other and pray for each other so that you may be healed. The prayer of a righteous person is powerful and effective.
>
> —James 5:14–16

An apostle is not required; healing never came from the apostles, only through them. Until Christ returns, every elder in any local church is authorized by God to pray for God to heal the sick—and God said He would answer.

Maybe this is a good time to share a few more of our children's encounters with God's gracious healing power.

Fifteen-year-old Kaliyah had been experiencing a lot of pain in her muscles, joints, and bones for several years. The doctor's initial diagnosis was simply growing pains. But a short time later she developed shin splints. At times the pain was so intense she was unable to stand on her feet.

Kaliyah bravely continued to try to live a normal teenage life and even remained on her school's track team. But the pain would be so debilitating following her track meets that she would go home with her legs wrapped in ice. Her mother could not bear to see her in so much pain, so they again visited the doctor. This time the doctor sent them to get blood work done. A week later they return to the doctor's office for the results, and Kaliyah's mom could tell something had changed.

The nurses and staff at the doctor's office were always nice, but they seemed to be especially gracious, even to the point of pity. When the doctor arrived with the test results, she handed them to Kaliyah's mother, Chartease. But before she could explain the findings, she was called out of the room for an emergency. Chartease read the papers she had been handed and saw the possible diagnosis: lupus.

"I closed my eyes, took a deep breath, and told myself, 'No,'" Chartease recalled.

When the doctor returned, she explained the diagnosis and what the next steps were.

"In my heart, I had already rebuked this thing that was attempting to work its way into our lives," Chartease says. "I told the doctor boldly that I was *not* claiming this for Kaliyah."

After the doctor left the room, one of the young ladies on the staff peeked her head in and asked, "Are y'all OK?" Chartease replied, "Girl, I have a lot of faith." The woman just smiled and closed the door.

That same week, our church hosted Girls Night In, an event put on by our women's ministry. Chartease spoke with my wife, Phyllis, about the situation, and Phyllis told her, "Oh, we're not worried about that. That's why we're here tonight." Phyllis told the rest of the women about Kaliyah's health concerns, and the youth spent that entire night praying and laying hands on Kaliyah. Chartease says she knew God moved in her daughter's life that night, and she no longer worried. When Kaliyah returned to the doctor, there was no diagnosis of lupus. Incredible![2]

If your children are sick, I want to encourage you to boldly pray for their healing. Please allow these testimonies from our church family to help to build your faith.

My greatest challenge in writing this chapter has not been what to say, but rather what not to say. There are so many scriptures and current accounts of God's healing power that it's difficult to choose which ones to focus upon.

I want to draw your attention to one final passage as we are building our faith to release and receive divine healing. Here we find God continuing to expand the scope and availability of healing to all.

First Corinthians 12 instructs us in the availability and operation of spiritual gifts. These gifts of the Holy Spirit enable the church—the believers, you and me—to truly be the present-day body of Christ through whom Jesus touches the world.

Throughout 1 Corinthians 12, the Greek word *charisma* is translated "gift" or "gifts." The root of this word is *charis*, or grace. How do these spiritual gifts, including the gift of healing, flow through common believers like you and me? By God's grace, His unearned favor. That means you qualify to pray for your child's health and healing. First Corinthians 12:7 declares that "to each one the manifestation of the Spirit is given." That includes you. Now and from now on, healing is available by the grace of God through anyone He may choose.

Pray for your children's healing. God will use you. Who said you need a white suit and a red tie to pray for the sick? I see healing being released by God's grace through an army wearing bathrobes, jogging suits, and blue jeans!

I want to share just one more healing testimony. It's not about a child; it's from one of the adults in our church. But it's just too good not to share.[3]

In July of 2008 Brenda was taken to the ER at a local hospital. She had no idea that the sudden blockage of her urinary tract was due to a large tumor. A doctor—the director of the cancer center, in fact—was called to the ER to look into Brenda's case. After his examination he was not even sure she would live long enough to be moved to the ICU.

She was diagnosed with uterine cancer. After further tests the results were shocking. She had stage four cancer, and initial tests revealed more than 250 metastasized cancer lesions on her lungs. She had four surgeries in the next two weeks just to attempt to stabilize her body for more cancer treatments. Brenda was told the survival rate for this type of cancer was only 3 to 7 percent.

After recovering from the surgeries, Brenda began chemo and radiation treatments. Her prognosis was not good; in fact, from all human and medical perspectives, it seemed nearly hopeless. But Jesus said, "For with God nothing will be impossible" (Luke 1:37, MEV).

Her husband was obviously overwhelmed with what they

had discovered. Yet in the midst of this walk through the valley of the shadow of death, God met him in a time of prayer and gave him great peace. John would hold on to this in the coming weeks. Of course, our church family and Brenda's family and friends were constantly praying.

Then it happened. A dear friend was driving Brenda home from one of her exhausting all-day chemo treatments. Brenda says her friend was trying to encourage her and engage her in conversation, but Brenda was so tired that she did not even have the energy to speak. All she could do in the face of her emotional and physical exhaustion was make one simple statement. She reached down deep inside and said, "I know that God is going to heal me." In that moment God invaded the car and Brenda's life. The ladies say God's presence literally exploded in the car. They almost pulled over to the shoulder. Everything changed that day. Healing had been released in Brenda's body, and cancer was no match.

Brenda has amazed her doctors, technicians, and nurses. In the fall of 2014, six years after her cancer diagnosis and her experience with God in the car, Brenda received another doctor's report: she is cancer-free. How great is our God!

LIVING IN DIVINE HEALTH

Before we close this chapter with some guidelines for how to pray for divine healing, let's not forget divine health. This is especially important as we develop a daily prayer strategy for our children.

What's the difference between praying for divine healing and divine health? We know that we pray for healing as a response to sickness. Praying for divine health, on the other hand, is proactive or preemptive. When we pray for divine health, we are asking God to protect us from sickness, disease, or injury. To be healed from a disease or illness is wonderful, but to be kept from the sickness would be even better.

Psalm 91 is our guideline for this kind of praying:

> Whoever dwells in the shelter of the Most High will rest in the shadow of the Almighty. I will say of the LORD, "He is my refuge and my fortress, my God, in whom I trust." Surely he will save you from the fowler's snare and from the deadly pestilence. He will cover you with his feathers, and under his wings you will find refuge; his faithfulness will be your shield and rampart. You will not fear the terror of night, nor the arrow that flies by day, nor the pestilence that stalks in the darkness, nor the plague that destroys at midday. A thousand may fall at your side, ten thousand at your right hand, but it will not come near you.
>
> —PSALM 91:1–7

In this psalm we are promised protection from disease and attack as we remain close to God. We are promised that God will be our "shield," and pestilence and plagues "will not come near" us. Can you see the power of praying daily that your children will live in divine health? Do you see the power in declaring God's promise that they are safe in the "shelter of the Most High" and in the "shadow of the Almighty"?

Psalm 91:9–10 tells us, "If you say, 'The LORD is my refuge,' and you make the Most High your dwelling, no harm will overtake you, no disaster will come near your tent." Consider what the *Spirit-Filled Life Bible* has to say about that passage: "When we make the Lord our refuge and habitation by trusting Him—taking our cares, fears and needs to Him; by seeking His counsel, spending times of refreshing with Him; and by loving Him and walking closely with Him through every day, we enter into a sheltered place of promise regarding health."[4]

I have experienced the power and protection of Psalm 91 personally. I was in Washington, DC, several years ago for the National Day of Prayer. It had been my privilege to join pastors and leaders from across the nation for two days of strategic planning and praying for revival in America. On the last day, I was planning to fly home that afternoon. Two pastors and another pastor and his wife joined me for a quick lunch before we would go our separate ways. Since we were close to the Capitol, we walked a few blocks and decided to eat at the ESPN Sports Zone Restaurant. (It's obvious that my friend's wife was outvoted on this one.) After having burgers and watching the games on the giant sports screens, my friends and I headed for the door to leave. But our plans changed very suddenly.

Armed guards, who were not at the door when we entered, told us we were not allowed to leave and that we should return to our table. No reason was given and no questions were answered. I thought, "Are you kidding me?" I was concerned that I would miss my flight. My friends and I returned to our table, but the once-animated buzz of a busy lunchtime restaurant had grown quiet.

Group after group returned to their tables, and no one really knew what was going on. Rumors began to fly from table to table. A bank had been robbed, and armed men were being pursued as they ran through the streets. Some foreign dignitary needed high security, and we were on lockdown.

No one really knew. Finally, after more than an hour, the restaurant manager made an announcement over the in-house sound system, and it was bad news—really bad news.

We were told that the restaurant was part of a larger federal office building, and the two shared a common air-conditioning system. While we were eating our lunch, an employee in one of the government offices was opening mail. When a certain envelope was opened, white powder spilled out, and the employee had an immediate reaction. This was during the time when anthrax-laced letters were being sent to government offices. Here we were, caught right in the crosshairs of this terrorist plot.

You can probably imagine how it felt to hear this unbelievable news. Anthrax can be transmitted through the air. Now we know why the guards were at the door. They were not protecting us; they were protecting the public *from* us! We were told that the powder was being tested, and no one could leave until they knew for sure what it was. The employee's immediate reaction to the powder had everyone in charge on high alert, and we just had to sit, wait, and wonder.

For a while no one said anything. What could we say? So many thoughts were racing through my head: "Have I really been poisoned by anthrax? Am I going to die? Am I going to be quarantined? Will I get to see my wife and daughters again?" No one was talking, but our thoughts were beating a deafening rhythm in our brains.

And then I did what I had learned to do in my relationship with Jesus Christ. I quietly began to pray. I was stunned by what was happening, but I knew God was still in control of my life. As I turned to God in this unthinkable moment,

His peace began to quiet my thoughts. Then I heard that familiar, quiet voice deep in my spirit. Yes, God was in control. He simply told me to start quoting Psalm 91.

I turned to my pastor-friends at the table with me and told them God wanted us to quote Psalm 91. No one questioned me. We just began to speak this great psalm out loud together. To be honest, I did not fully realize what was about to happen. I was still rattled, but I was obedient. When we got to verse 6, the light came on. When we said we would not fear "the plague that destroys at midday," we all stopped. That was it. We had just received a *rhema* word from God—a right-now promise. God had walked into the valley of the shadow of death with us and told us we were coming out on the other side.

We were not going to be healed from anthrax—we were actually being protected from it. It was "midday," and the "plague" would not come near us! With this Holy Spirit–inspired promise now ours, everything changed again. We received an amazing peace that only God could have given. People were crying, fearful, angry, and confused, and understandably so. But at our table, we were now smiling and humbly overwhelmed with gratitude, even while we waited to hear the results.

After more than two hours, the manager finally spoke again. He was very sorry for our inconvenience. Although the white powder initially presented all the characteristics of anthrax, it had tested negative. So we were free to go. I will never know what that powder really was or whether God changed it from something harmful to something harmless. What I do know is that I have never seen that kind of fear or government security in place. And I know that when God promises to protect us from illness, He is able to do just that. I believe God worked miraculously, even though I don't know exactly what He did behind the scenes.

These are the promises I hold close to my heart as I pray for my children's and grandchildren's health. I have included the following "prayer starter" for you to use as a guide as you intercede each day for your children's health:

> *Father, in Jesus's name, I thank You today that my child is walking in divine health. I ask You keep him under the shadow of Your wing, safe from all sickness or attack, according to Psalm 91. I ask that Your angels encamp around my child today, according to Psalm 34:7. I pray that no virus, germ, or bacteria will enter his body. I declare that my child's immune system operates supernaturally by the power of Your Holy Spirit. I apply the unequaled blood Jesus Christ shed victoriously on the cross to cover my child. Just as You did for Israel in Egypt, death, disease, and destruction will have to pass over my child and not touch him at all. I pray that every organ and organ system will develop fully and operate perfectly. I also thank You that he is protected from all falls, injuries, wounds, or attacks. I thank You that my child is walking in divine health and safety. In Jesus's name, amen.*

If the time comes to pray for their healing, you will be ready. I encourage you to pray something like this:

> *Father, in Jesus's name, I bring my child before You. I ask "by faith in the name of Jesus" (Acts 3:16) that You heal him now. I believe that by the stripes Jesus received on His back healing was secured for this moment, as 1 Peter 2:24 says. I ask that gifts of healing and miracles would be released to heal my child's body at this very moment because of Your promise in 1 Corinthians 12:9–10. I thank You that healing is Your gift and Your will. I declare that sickness must leave and not return to my child. Let Your kingdom come and Your will be done here and now on earth. Let Your name be glorified. In Jesus's name, amen.*

Wow! You are really getting into this. I can sense your faith growing by leaps and bounds. The next area of prayer concerns your child's ability to learn and excel in his or her education. Let's keep moving.

Chapter 4

PRAYER PRINCIPLE #2: EDUCATIONAL EXCELLENCE AND DEVELOPMENT

...showing aptitude for every kind of learning, well informed, quick to understand.

—DANIEL 1:4

THE CATALYST FOR the entire Daniel Prayer model was my passion to see Christian children flourish in their educational environments. Every parent knows the incredible value of a great education. A good education positions a child for many wonderful opportunities in life, and it is one of the most valuable gifts parents can give their children.

But there are significant challenges facing students in today's public schools. As I mentioned earlier, our church is very supportive of our local schools. I am blessed to work with and personally know many godly educators, and I know they are making a tremendous impact on children's lives in public schools. But I also know that biblical values and truths have deteriorated in our society, and this has impacted our public education system.

Schoolchildren spend at least thirty hours every week in a classroom. Other than sleeping, this is probably the largest block of time in their weekly schedule. These hours are shaping and impacting their lives. This is why we must pray. To send our children to school without covering them in prayer would be a big mistake.

Schools do not always affirm the values you teach at home, but that doesn't mean your child's educational experience can't be a blessing and a joy. Daniel excelled in his education while in Babylon, and it positioned him to use his public service as a platform to promote his unshakable faith in God. I am convinced that God's plan for every child is to enjoy an education that is as successful as Daniel's. As you pray for your children each day, your prayer of faith will go before them and open the right doors—the God-planned doors—and close the ones that would be detrimental to God's purpose for their lives.

The Bible says Daniel showed aptitude for every kind of learning. He was well-informed and quick to understand. Not all children are gifted in the same areas, but all children are capable of flourishing in their educational environment. No matter where our children begin their educational journeys, and no matter what obstacles they may face, I am confident that they can excel in their education.

As we pray that our children will have "aptitude for every kind of learning" and that they are "quick to understand," God will show us how to best help them respond to the challenges they face in school and make the most of their God-given gifts. He will give us discernment about how they learn best. And our faith will grow as we ask and believe for God to develop any area in which our children may be struggling.

I have seen God's faithfulness to do this in the life of one of my own grandchildren. She was and is today one of the kindest, most gentle-spirited people I know. I knew God had made her to fulfill a very important purpose in His kingdom.

We were all so excited for her to begin kindergarten and take the first step in her education but, boy, were we in for a shock! Within the first nine weeks of kindergarten, her teacher gave her mother a stunning evaluation of my granddaughter's progress and potential. We were told that she had severe learning disabilities and that ultimately she would need to be placed on medication.

We were completely caught off guard. We were aware of a slight speech impediment, and she was receiving speech therapy to help her in that area. But that was it. We had seen no other signs to indicate what we were now hearing.

The teacher told us that she would not be able to read and would have to repeat kindergarten—all of this in the first nine weeks. We were, of course, devastated. We didn't know what we should do—or what we could do.

There wasn't much "we" could do, but there was a lot that God could do. So we prayed—a lot. I watched my wife pray. I listened to my daughter and her family pray. They have all taught me how to pray at greater levels of faith, and I hope the testimonies of answered prayer in this book will do the same for you.

After we prayed, we discussed how we should respond to the information we had been given and how best to support our granddaughter. We were fully connected and concerned, and we were not in denial. But we could not just accept this bad news as a final diagnosis. After much prayer, we chose to not accept the labels that were being placed on our little one. We decided to pray like nothing but prayer could change things, and to reach out to any resource that might help our grandchild learn to the best of our ability.

At the end of a challenging year, her parents decided not to hold her back in kindergarten but to move her along to first grade. I praise God for her first-grade teacher; she truly was an answer to our prayers. She gave our granddaughter a chance to start first grade with no preconceived ideas about her abilities. She pulled our granddaughter out of her very timid shell and recognized the academic gifts and learning pace that others had missed. As tough as kindergarten had been for her, first grade was a delight. She began to flourish academically. She quickly caught up with her reading level and continues to this day to excel in reading. We were and are so thankful that no medication was ever required.

My granddaughter has never looked back. She has been on the A–B honor roll from that time on. She was on the leadership team in elementary school and led several school assemblies, and she continues to do well now that she is in middle school. She shared short sermons (she didn't get the "short" part from me) in our church's children's ministries and is doing the same now in her junior high student ministries group.[1]

God is faithful! Can I get an amen? You see, faith in God is not denial. We saw the circumstances, but we knew that God was not confined by those circumstances. Sometimes life can bring some very bad news. But don't give up. Wait for God to give you a second opinion.

Let's take the limits off our understanding of God and begin to pray bigger, bolder prayers for our children. God will not be intimidated and neither should we. Our children deserve nothing less than our persistent prayers, and the mountains blocking their educational development will be moved by nothing less.

THE FOUNDATION OF A GREAT EDUCATION

It only makes sense to bring our children's educational needs to God. He is the source of all wisdom and understanding. God can take our children further in their intellectual development than we could ever imagine. The Bible says, "The fear of the LORD is the beginning of knowledge" (Prov. 1:7, MEV). Knowing this truth is a must in understanding God, prayer, and intellectual development.

To fear the Lord as Proverbs instructs is not to be in slavish terror of some oppressive tyrant. It means to have reverence, respect, even awe. This is the beginning of knowledge; it is where all knowledge originates. This respect and trust in God is the foundation for a truly great education. There is more to education than just the accumulation of facts.

We saw in Proverbs 1:7 that the fear of the Lord releases knowledge. But notice that Proverbs 9:10 tells us that the fear of the Lord is also the beginning of wisdom. What's the difference? Knowledge and wisdom are the twins of education. Simply put, knowledge is the accumulation of facts, and wisdom is the ability to know what to do with those facts.

In the introductory notes to the Book of Proverbs, the *Spirit-Filled Life Bible* says wisdom is the ability to judge and act according to God's directives. It "originates in God, not self, and comes by attention to instruction." Wisdom and righteousness go together; it's good to be wise and wise to be good.[2]

Wisdom and knowledge do not just include God; He is their source. As we lead our children into a personal relationship with Christ, which we will discuss in the next chapter, we are actually introducing them to the Author of all knowledge.

The connection between God and education is dynamic. There are, of course, many highly intelligent nonbelievers who have accomplished great things and received numerous accolades in their fields. Their knowledge has been a great resource. However, as we consider God's best for our children, we must remember that knowledge alone is not enough.

Gaining godly wisdom to guide our knowledge is the highest education. Biblically based education always includes having the wisdom and understanding to properly apply knowledge. Everyone can see the stars, but godly wisdom enables us to see the God who made the stars.

With this understanding in mind, you may want to begin praying along these lines for your child: "Lord, I thank You and declare that my daughter is walking in the fear of the Lord. She is growing in reverence and respect of You and Your Word. She is in awe of You and willingly obeys Your Word. Because of this, she is now growing and developing in wisdom and knowledge."

Are you getting this? Begin to add what you are learning here to your prayer time. Implement these truths. Remember, God has never answered a prayer that has not been prayed.

GOD CAN TAKE THE LIMITS OFF

Your child's ability to learn is greater than you can imagine, and God is the One who can unlock the unique way in which he or she will grow intellectually. This is why we pray.

Consider the unequaled wisdom that God gave Solomon. Solomon is considered one of the wisest men, if not the wisest man, who ever lived. And his wisdom came as an answer to prayer! In 1 Kings 3:5 we read that God appeared to the young king in a dream. What God told him in that encounter was stunning. God gave Solomon a blank check from heaven with His signature affixed. God said, "Ask for whatever you want Me to give you." Can you imagine?

What was Solomon's request? "Give your servant a discerning heart to govern your people and to distinguish between right and wrong" (1 Kings 3:9). The Lord was pleased that Solomon had asked for this, so God said to him, "I will do what you have asked. I will give you a wise and discerning heart, so that there will never have been anyone like you, nor will there ever be" (1 Kings 3:12).

The Bible tells us, "God gave Solomon wisdom and very great insight, and a breadth of understanding as measureless as the sand on the seashore" (1 Kings 4:29). That was one smart man. A prayer for the wisdom of God opened Solomon up to unprecedented educational advancement.

I hope you make the connection here. The Bible says that God is no respecter of persons. He is able to answer your prayer for your child just as He did for Solomon. Solomon desired the wisdom of God, and he applied himself, but God took the limits off. I'm convinced that your prayers can have the same effect.

The more you pray for your child's educational advancement, the more effective your prayers will become. As you pray, you will gain insight into your child's needs, and you will begin to discern how to motivate and encourage your child. God will reveal His purposes and provision for your child, and this knowledge will make your prayers more specific and dynamic.

Your child's educational development is directly connected to your prayer life. And there are no limits on prayer.

When I was in Bible college, I witnessed one of the greatest examples of how God's presence can affect a person's education. I had met two great guys who were both former drug addicts. They had been saved through the ministry of Teen Challenge and later sensed God's call into the ministry, so they entered Bible college to prepare for the future.

The challenge was their previous education—or lack thereof. These two young men were obviously passionate followers of Christ and very intelligent. But their former life of drug addiction had caused them to drop out of school. Now here they were, enrolled in a small Bible college with some pretty high academic standards. From a purely human perspective, it seemed they might not make it through the program. But they prayed.

Both young men graduated from Bible college and entered the ministry. How did they do it? They prayed and began to memorize God's Word, and as they did this, day by day they could see their aptitude changing. They once told me it was like the fog of drug abuse began to lift off their brains. Little by little they began to read better and retain more of what they read. They said the Word of God began to wash their minds and restore their ability to learn. It was a process, slow at first, but powerful in its healing restoration.

Maybe as you read this today, your child is struggling with a learning disability. It is so important that you know God has a specific plan for your child. Every child in every circumstance matters to God, and there are no exceptions to His promises. When God said, "For I know the plans I have for you…plans to prosper you and not to harm you, plans to give you hope and a future" (Jer. 29:11), He meant it. God's plans and purposes include wonderful children who have special needs, and He is just as concerned about their educational growth and excellence as He is any other student's.

If you have a special-needs child or one struggling with a learning disability, be faithful to pray for your child daily, and you will begin to see just how faithful God is to develop him. Your child's path may be different and his challenges and victories unique, but every success is significant.

Sometimes God will answer your prayer for your child's learning challenge by sending the right person. My wife and I know a wonderful woman who teaches students with learning difficulties. I want to share just a few testimonies she recently sent to us.

One of her students, a young lady who had been diagnosed with dyslexia in math and reading, was recently named one of the top ten students in her junior college. This young lady was told by her sixth-grade teacher that she would never be college material. But God!

Another student has been receiving high As in her college English assignments. And yet another student who could not put more than a couple of sentences together when this teacher began working with him now can write full essays.

Isn't that incredible? These students haven't excelled merely because of our friend's abilities as a teacher. She prays daily for her students by name. "I know this makes all the difference in the world," she said. "To Him be the glory!"[3]

Can God change the course of your child's educational journey? Absolutely. Can every child improve, grow, and develop? Without a doubt. I believe that your consistent, daily prayer for your children's educational excellence and development will open doors for them that you may never have imagined. God may sovereignly increase your child's ability, He may send a gifted teacher who understands how she learns, or He may do both—or something greater than you even know how to ask for.

THE EPHESIANS 3:20 PRINCIPLE

The wonderful thing about faithful prayer is that the all-powerful God is on the other side of the equation. When we have done all we know to do, God will do all that we cannot imagine. When we do what we can—pray—God will do what we cannot.

This is the Ephesians 3:20 prayer principle: we pray and then let God take over. We must ask, seek, and knock, and then let God finish the story. As Ephesians 3:20 states, God "is able to do exceedingly abundantly beyond all that we ask or imagine, according to the power that works in us" (MEV). As we pray for our children, God is able to do "immeasurably more than all we ask or imagine." What a comfort—and what a motivation to pray.

God is with you and for your children as you pray for their educational development and excellence. Remember, the Bible doesn't tell us that Solomon was born a genius. His wisdom was an answer to prayer.

Every child is unique. They all learn in different ways. They respond to different models and approaches, and each child has different constraints and weaknesses. It's important to recognize what is your child's best and celebrate his or her progress.

Let me tell you a little about Jonathan.[4] He is a very special young man who is overachieving in his life. It has been my delight to observe his progress. But his parents had to learn how to encourage him through some difficult challenges.

At a young age, Jonathan was diagnosed with a type of autism called Asperger's syndrome as well as dyslexia. Asperger's affects Jonathan's social skills, and dyslexia affects his ability to read and transfer information from his short-term memory to his long-term memory.

Jonathan was home-schooled for several years, but during that time he went to public school for speech therapy and to participate in a group that helped him work on his social skills. Typically Jonathan would separate himself from whatever was going on. In Sunday school, he would go to class, but he would sit under the table. His Sunday school teacher would acknowledge him and invite him to participate in class activities but not make him come out of his comfort zone. Yet over time, as Jonathan grew comfortable with the environment, he began to sit at the table and participate.

Jonathan's parents said God has always placed the right programs and people in his path to help him overcome the challenges of autism and dyslexia. He always put people in their son's life who would encourage him. Because of God's faithfulness, Jonathan graduated from high school and is currently working on a drafting degree in college.

God is able to take any child at any point and impact his education. Just begin praying right where you are. Just start. Your faith will grow. Your understanding and discernment of your child and how to pray for him will grow.

Our children's education will greatly impact the rest of

their lives. Our daily prayers for them will allow God to help them take this journey with the best results. He will develop in them knowledge, wisdom, and godly character and prepare them for the great things He has planned for their lives. Remember, God answers prayer. God honors prayer. And prayer changes things.

As you intercede for your children's educational excellence and intellectual development, I encourage you to pray along these lines:

> *Father, I thank You for this wonderful, unique child You have entrusted to me. Today I pray that You will give him aptitude for every kind of learning, that he will be well informed and quick to understand every subject that he will be taught. I ask You to give my child the ability to listen, concentrate, and understand every teacher in every class. I thank You that nothing is too hard for him. I pray that You will help my child develop in any area in which he struggles. I pray that my child is respectful and attentive in every class. I thank You that he will comprehend and retain everything he is taught. I thank You, God, the Author of all wisdom and knowledge, that You are releasing Your ability within my child today! In Jesus's name I pray, amen.*

I'm excited about the educational growth of your child. I can't wait to see how God will answer your prayers. But there are more principles to cover, and this next prayer focus is truly the most important one of all.

Chapter 5

PRAYER PRINCIPLE #3:
A RESOLVE TO SERVE GOD

*But Daniel resolved not to defile himself
with the royal food and wine.*

—DANIEL 1:8

YOU MAY REMEMBER the story. Daniel had been handpicked to serve the king, and he was to be given food and wine from the king's table. But Daniel refused to indulge. Why? Was eating the king's food really such a big deal? In a word, *yes!*

Daniel had resolved that no matter what he faced in Babylon, he would continue to serve his God. His circumstances would not cause him to compromise his faith.

How could eating the king's food cause him to compromise? I'm glad you asked. It was customary in Babylon during Daniel's time for the king's meat to have first been offered to a demonic idol before it was eaten. Daniel knew this, and it would have been a violation of his conscience and his faith to eat food or drink sacrificed to idols. Daniel was determined that nothing would come between him and his God.

The prayer focus we will discuss in this chapter is the most important one of all. It is the center of the five facets of the Daniel Prayer, and it should be the center of your prayers for your children. Seeing your children come into a personal relationship with Jesus Christ should be the pinnacle of your prayer life because it is the greatest gift you could ever give them.

Praying for our children to resolve to serve God begins with asking Him to give them a firsthand revelation of Jesus Christ. They must encounter Him for themselves and make their own decision to accept Christ as their Savior. A secondhand faith—relying on their parents' faith instead of their own—will not cut it in this culture. Daniel had to stand on his own relationship with God. When his faith was challenged, he was able to remain firm because of his own commitment to follow God, not because of his parents' or grandparents' faith.

Only a personal relationship with God will give our children that kind of resolve. Spiritually speaking, God has no grandchildren, just children. The baton of personal faith must be passed to each succeeding generation. They cannot rely on our relationship with God. They must develop one for themselves.

When our children must stand alone, when they have to make a decision to be faithful to God when it's not easy or popular, their strength will be drawn only from the well of their own personal faith. The resolve to serve God is a product of a person's relationship with Him.

But I encourage you to think of it this way: God has entrusted you with a high and holy calling as a parent. You are the vessel He has chosen to introduce your child to the incomparable gift of salvation. God trusts you with this task, and He has equipped and enabled you to do it. As a parent, you are anointed as both intercessor and evangelist for your child.

As Christian parents we want to see a chain of generational faith in our families. There are several examples of this chain of faith in Scripture. Consider Paul's young protégé,

Timothy. The apostle wrote in his letter to Timothy, "I am reminded of your sincere faith, which first lived in your grandmother Lois and in your mother Eunice and, I am persuaded, now lives in you also" (2 Tim. 1:5). At some point the genuine faith of the preceding generations became real and personal for Timothy, and he began to walk out his own relationship with Christ as a minister of the gospel. The prayers of previous generations were being answered in and through Timothy—and not only was Timothy saved, but others came to Christ through his witness.

Moses is another example of the chain of generational faith at work. The Bible says, "By faith Moses' parents hid him for three months after he was born, because they saw he was no ordinary child, and they were not afraid of the king's edict" (Heb. 11:23). It took some courageous faith and devotion to God's purpose for Moses's parents to take such a risk.

We know that Pharaoh had given the unthinkable decree that all the male babies born to the Israelites were to be executed at birth. To violate his order would be a death sentence for the parents as well. I imagine that reluctantly and tearfully the Israelite parents surrendered to Pharaoh's wicked attempt at genocide. But not Moses's mom and dad.

Two core values are operating in this account. First, Moses's parents trusted God more than they feared man. That, again, is the fruit of a personal relationship with God. Secondly, they "saw that he was no ordinary child" and were devoted at all costs to seeing God's purpose for their son's life fulfilled. That kind of a passionate commitment to God creates an atmosphere for children to make the same connection with Him.

How would their prayer and example influence Moses when his time to choose came? The Bible says:

> By faith Moses, when he had grown up, refused to be known as the son of Pharaoh's daughter. He chose to be mistreated along with the people of God rather than to enjoy the fleeting pleasures of sin. He regarded disgrace for the sake of Christ as of greater value than the treasures of Egypt, because he was looking ahead to his reward.
> —HEBREWS 11:24–26

That's what I would call resolve. What an incredible choice by a young man of faith. I would say that his parents gave him an inheritance that money could neither buy nor produce. God wants you to do the same for your children. Before we go any further, I urge you to pray the following prayer:

> Lord, I ask You to make me a parent who lives a life of faith and sets a godly example for my children. Help me to trust You more than I fear any man. Enable me to recognize and cooperate with Your plan for my children at all costs. Help me to pray daily for their salvation. In Jesus's name, amen.

I believe God wants to build up your confidence that you can set a godly example for your children and lead them to faith in Christ. Trust me, your words and actions will not go unnoticed.

Moses's parents began their "faith with actions" commitment the moment their son was born. They may have even decided to disobey Pharaoh's orders before he was born. Either way, I believe their example shows us that it's never too early to begin to pray for your child's salvation. Children can be born again. Children are capable of making a decision to follow Christ. Never underestimate their young hearts' ability to respond to the gospel.

It was important to Jesus that children be allowed to come to Him. We read in the Gospel of Matthew:

> Then little children were brought to Him that He might put His hands on them and pray. But the disciples rebuked them. But Jesus said, "Let the little children come to Me, and do not forbid them. For to such belongs the kingdom of heaven." He laid His hands on them and departed from there.
>
> —MATTHEW 19:13–15, MEV

The only timing mistake you can make in introducing your children to Jesus is waiting too long. We all rejoice to hear the testimonies of men and women who were saved and delivered from sin and bondage—and rightly so. Yet what we often overlook in these wonderful examples of God's grace are the years that were lost in sin. Those years cannot be relived. But when a child is born again, he has his entire life to give to God. This is the greatest of testimonies, and this is what we are praying for. I believe that if God is able to save you from it, He can also keep you from it.

UNSHAKABLE FAITH

Never underestimate the power of God working in and through a child. Take Samuel as an example. His mother, Hannah, had been unable to conceive, and she was desperate to have a child. While praying, she promised God that if He enabled her to have a son, she would give the boy back to Him. God answered her prayer, and Hannah kept her word.

Samuel was very young when his mother gave him to Eli the priest. Samuel would now grow up in the priesthood and live with Eli his entire life. This may seem like an incredible testimony, until we find out about Eli's family. Shockingly, we read that his sons were also in the priesthood, but their lifestyle was hardly something Hannah would want her son to emulate. The Bible says, "Eli's sons were wicked men; they had no regard for the LORD" (1 Sam. 2:12, HCSB). Young Samuel had entered into a dysfunctional train wreck.

The Bible did not exaggerate. Eli's two sons were indeed wicked. They stole some of the offerings that were brought to be offered to God, and they even used their position and influence to commit sexual sins with the women who served at the entrance to the Tent of Meeting. It seems that even though Eli was aware of their behavior, he was unable or unwilling to stop them.

Yet amazingly, we read this about the young Samuel, who lived in the midst of a spiritual Twilight Zone: "Now the boy Samuel was growing both in stature and favor with the LORD and also with men" (1 Sam. 2:26, MEV). That's certainly a testament to the power of God at work in young Samuel's life!

When Samuel was growing up in the priesthood, the Bible says "the word of the LORD was rare; there were not many visions" (1 Sam. 3:1). I can see that happening. Why would God talk with priests who were wicked and unfaithful to Him? Eli and his sons were totally failing God, so He decided to raise up someone else.

One night while Samuel was lying down in the temple

of the Lord, God spoke to him. At first, Samuel struggled to recognize God's voice. He was young and just coming to understand how God would speak to him. But this began his training as a prophet of God. I can't help but wonder what would have happened to the priesthood without this boy. It may very well have dissolved. It could be that God's plan for Samuel was much bigger than either Hannah or Eli even realized. Samuel may have been chosen not just to be God's prophet but to save the priesthood. And He began unfolding His plan when Samuel was still just a child.

I encourage you to take a second look at those children or grandchildren in your life. God's plans for them just may be much bigger than anything you have dared to dream. As you intercede for their relationship with Christ, you are praying that God will work in their lives at the highest level, even beyond your own dreams for them.

Samuel managed to maintain an unshakable faith in the midst of the dysfunctional situation in which he grew up, and that is exactly what we should believe for our children— that their faith would remain steadfast and unmovable in the midst of a culture in chaos.

Samuel was God's instrument to guard the spiritual direction of an entire nation—and I'm convinced that there are some world-changers in your home right now playing with Barbie dolls or video games. I assure you that they're not too young for you to pray that God will be with them, just as He was with Samuel. The Bible says:

> The LORD was with Samuel as he grew up, and he
> let none of Samuel's words fall to the ground. And
> all Israel from Dan to Beersheba recognized that

> Samuel was attested as a prophet of the LORD. The
> LORD continued to appear at Shiloh, and there he
> revealed himself to Samuel through his word. And
> Samuel's word came to all Israel.
>
> —1 SAMUEL 3:19–4:1

Samuel remained faithful to God, and God was faithful to complete the work He began in Samuel when he was just a little boy. He will do the same for our children as they resolve to live for Him.

IT'S NEVER TOO LATE

Of course, your children's spiritual journey must have a starting point. God's purpose and destiny for them is released the moment that they accept Christ as their Savior. You can be sure that your prayer for your children's salvation is even more important to God than it is to you. When you pray for their salvation, you step into an unshakable partnership with God—because He has promised to answer this prayer.

Acts 16:31 says, "Believe in the Lord Jesus, and you will be saved—you and your household." And we read in 1 Timothy 2:3–4, "This is good, and pleases God our Savior, who wants all people to be saved and to come to a knowledge of the truth."

It is God's will that your children be saved and come into the knowledge of the truth. When you pray for your child's salvation, you are not pleading with God to do something He doesn't really want to do. You are declaring, in the authority of Jesus's name, that His will be done on earth. What happens when you pray in agreement with God's will? "This is the confidence we have in approaching God: that if we ask anything according to his will, he hears us. And if we know that he hears us—whatever we ask—we know that we have what we asked of him" (1 John 5:14–15).

Maybe your child has already become a teenager or young adult. Remember that God's promises and your prayers are unlimited. It's never too late to begin praying for your children to be saved. If they are your children, God is determined to reach them and make them His as well.

Maybe your child was raised in a godly home but is not serving the Lord at this time. Perhaps he has turned his back on you and God. Don't be discouraged. Isaiah 43 always reminds me that our children are never too far, and that it is never too late.

> Since you are precious and honored in my sight, and because I love you, I will give people in exchange for you, nations in exchange for your life. Do not be afraid, for I am with you; I will bring your children from the east and gather you from the west. I will say to the north, "Give them up!" and to the south, "Do not hold them back." Bring my sons from afar and my daughters from the ends of the earth—everyone who is called by my name, whom I created for my glory, whom I formed and made.
> —Isaiah 43:4–7

Remember this promise and let it encourage you as you pray for your children today. When you're in prayer, you are able to see what you could not see otherwise. As you pray consistently, the eyes of your faith will become clearer and clearer. There are moments in each of our lives when we feel surrounded and trapped by our cares and burdens. Right now your prodigal son or daughter may seem so far from

God that it looks hopeless. You just cannot "see" how anything can change.

The prophet Elisha's servant had a moment like this. He knew his life and Elisha's were in danger. The king of Aram was determined to capture Elisha, and he sent his army to apprehend him.

This was the day Elisha's servant had been dreading. When the servant of the man of God got up and went out early the next morning, an army with horses and chariots had surrounded the city. "Oh no, my lord! What shall we do?" the servant asked (2 Kings 6:15). But there was something Elisha's servant had not seen.

> "Don't be afraid," the prophet answered. "Those who are with us are more than those who are with them." And Elisha prayed, "Open his eyes, LORD, so that he may see." Then the LORD opened the servant's eyes, and he looked and saw the hills full of horses and chariots of fire all around Elisha."
>
> —2 KINGS 6:16–17

Did you catch that? Those who are with us are more than those who are with them. God is on your side in this spiritual tug-of-war for your child. Keep praying, my friend. I believe God wants you to "see" something that He has been seeing all along, and I believe God wants you to hear some things you have not heard before too.

As I write this, I'm beginning to hear footsteps. They seem to be coming from the north and the south, from the east and from the west. Those unsaved children, those who have run away—they are coming home. They are coming back to Christ. Things may not "look" or "sound" any different on the outside, but ask God to help you see and hear your children coming in by faith. They are much too close for you to stop praying now.

When you get discouraged, remind yourself of these promises God has made concerning our children. He is faithful, and He keeps His promises. God says:

> Yes, captives will be taken from warriors, and plunder retrieved from the fierce; I will contend with those who contend with you, and your children I will save.
>
> —Isaiah 49:25

> All your children will be taught by the Lord, and great will be their peace.
>
> —Isaiah 54:13

> "As for me, this is my covenant with them," says the Lord. "My Spirit, who is on you, will not depart from you, and my words that I have put in your mouth will always be on your lips, on the lips of your children and on the lips of their descendants—from this time on and forever," says the Lord.
>
> —Isaiah 59:21

> So the next generation would know them, even the children yet to be born, and they in turn would tell their children.
>
> —Psalm 78:6

> But from everlasting to everlasting the Lord's love is with those who fear him, and his righteousness with their children's children.
>
> —Psalm 103:17

I declare right now that your children and grandchildren will serve the Lord, and they will impact their generation just as Daniel did.

THREE KEYS TO DANIEL'S RESOLVE

We began this chapter talking about Daniel's example of faith and trust in God. This is what we want to see in our children. As I prepare to close this chapter, I want to take a closer look at three qualities that helped Daniel remain firm in his resolve to serve the Lord. I believe that understanding these attributes will greatly influence how we pray for our children.

Daniel made a decision to follow God.

First, as we read in Daniel 1:8, Daniel "resolved" not to defile himself. As we have discussed throughout this chapter, the most important thing we can pray for our children is that they come to know Jesus Christ as their personal Savior. That is the genesis, the beginning, of a blessed life. Then when they have received the precious gift of salvation, we must pray that they remain faithful to God, and grow and develop in their faith.

When we pray that our children are resolved to follow Christ, it means we're praying that they make a firm decision to live for God. This is not something we can do for them. They must own this choice.

Daniel had a sense of purpose.

To be resolved also means to have a firmness of purpose. In fact, the King James Version says Daniel "purposed in his heart that he would not defile himself with the portion of the king's meat" (1:8). So the second trait we see in Daniel is that though he was young, he already had a sense of purpose for his life. One of the most valuable assets in keeping on track to fulfill your goals and stay true to your values is knowing that God has a purpose for your life. With God's purpose at the forefront of his mind, Daniel refused to turn from the Lord's direction for his life.

Purpose also gave Daniel a sense of identity and value. It gave him the perspective that allowed him to make good choices in tough times. Give your children a sense of purpose. Help them see that they are uniquely created by God with an original destiny. Help them understand that God designed them to fulfill a purpose that is theirs alone. As they mature and develop in their own walk with Christ, this purpose will become more and more clear to them. But it will help them tremendously to hear you remind them of their purpose and their potential—and to hear you praying that they would walk fully in the things God has purposed for their lives.

Daniel was willing to go against the flow.

For Daniel, resolving to be true to God was more than a mental assent. He didn't decide to just follow God quietly and not make waves with the king. He went public with his convictions when he refused to eat from the king's table. Our children may not be offered food sacrificed to idols, but they will have plenty of opportunities to give in to peer pressure. When they are resolved to serve the Lord, they will be able to go against the flow and do what pleases God, not their peers.

I imagine that all parents in the history of mankind have heard their children say, "But everybody's doing it." From our reading of Daniel chapter 1, it seems that only Daniel and his three friends had the resolve to refuse the king's food. Out of all of the young exiles from Israel, it would seem they were the only ones who chose to go against the flow.

Going out of step with one's friends is never easy, and the younger you are the harder it is. Daniel seemed to be the leader of this quartet of nonconformists, and that's what we are praying our children will be—the influencers and not the influenced. That is the third quality I want to draw your attention to: Daniel was young, but he was a strong leader. There are tons of books on leadership, but I can tell you one thing about leadership that I know to be true: great leaders of men are first followers of Christ. We want to pray that our children will refuse the easy path—and lead others to do the same.

I've said it often in this book: this Daniel Prayer strategy is not designed to help our children to merely survive. We want our children to overcome, excel, influence, and lead. God has big plans for them, and that is why we must pray big prayers over them.

As I said previously, I don't want to give you a formula so you can pray for your children by rote. But I encourage you to use the following prayer as a guide for interceding for your child's relationship with Christ.

> *I thank You, Father, that You sent Your Son to become our Savior. My prayer today is that my child will come to know Jesus as his personal Savior. I pray that at the earliest age possible he will understand his need for Christ. I pray that You will open my child's heart and understanding to the gospel, and that he will experience the*

wonderful grace of God for himself. I thank You that it is Your will for my child to be born again and filled with the Holy Spirit.

I pray that my child will not only come into a personal relationship with You, but that he will then resolve and purpose to follow You. I pray he will not give in to the pressures of friends and culture. I pray that he will recognize and refuse everything and anyone that would pull him away from Your purpose. I thank You that my child is a leader as he follows You.

Finally, I pray that You will empower me to live such a life before my child that he will become hungry to know You personally. Give me the wisdom and sensitivity to know when and how to lead him to You. In Jesus's name I pray, amen.

I'm convinced that as you pray, God will give you wisdom and opportunities to share your faith and lead your children to salvation. Resolving to follow Christ is the most important decision they will ever make. Nothing is more important for their future. When your children begin to walk closely with God, they will not only grow in their resolve to serve the Lord, they will be positioned to experience the next aspect of the Daniel Prayer: divine favor.

Chapter 6

PRAYER PRINCIPLE #4:
DIVINE FAVOR

*Now God had caused the official to show
favor and compassion to Daniel.*

—DANIEL 1:9

THROUGHOUT SCRIPTURE, THERE is a principle that opens doors, breaks through any barrier, positions for promotion, and accelerates one into the timing of God. That principle is the favor of God. Daniel received divine favor at a critical moment in his life, and it positioned him for a life of uncommon influence.

As we read in the previous chapter, Daniel had decided not to eat from the king's table. When he told the official that he did not want to defile himself by eating food sacrificed to idols, the king's official could have responded harshly, punishing Daniel and his friends. But that's not what happened. The Bible says God caused the official to show Daniel favor, and because of that divine favor, Daniel convinced him to wait and see how he and his friends looked after eating vegetables and drinking water for ten days.

The official agreed to the test, and after the ten days Daniel and his friends "looked healthier and better nourished than any of the young men who ate the royal food" (Dan. 1:15). From that point on, Daniel was no longer pressured to eat from the king's table, and those around him saw God's supernatural work in his life. That's the power of divine favor.

Your child must receive the favor of God to live at the highest level. But I am convinced that we cannot pray in faith for our children to receive this blessing until we truly understand the purposes and principles of favor. We must know what we are asking for if we are to recognize it when it comes.

Favor is like a divine current that picks you up in your present position and carries you into your place of promise. Favor is that which connects you to what seemed impossible. Someone once said that one day of favor is greater than a lifetime of labor. How true!

God releases His favor in His timing upon the people of destiny. It is a gift of God, and we can't earn it or deserve it—but we should seek it for our children in prayer. Favor releases God's power and provision. Favor will position you to be at the right place at the right time with all you need to do the right thing. Can you see why you must pray every day that your children will have this?

When God's favor comes upon a person, it positions him to fulfill his purpose. Very often favor will come from unexpected sources in unexpected places. This is what happened to a young Jewish girl named Esther.

Esther was an exile in a foreign country just as Daniel was. Evidently her parents died in the attack on Israel, because she ended up in the care of her godly cousin Mordecai, who also lived in the royal city of Susa.

Just as she was adjusting to life in this strange land, a series of events occurred that would forever change her life. King Xerxes became angry with his queen and banished her from the palace to a place of obscurity. Upon the counsel of his trusted officials, the king initiated a search throughout the kingdom for a new queen.

The beautiful young Esther was forced into this royal version of *The Bachelor*. I imagine she must have been frightened to be conscripted into this parade of potential partners for the king. She was separated from Mordecai and made to move into the palace with the other candidates, a stranger to everyone there.

A lot of people think of Esther's story as a fairy tale, but I doubt it felt like that to this young Jewish girl. She was a foreigner in the king's palace. How would her faith in God survive in such a place? How would *she* survive?

Esther, of course, did not know what God had in store for her. But in the midst of what seemed to be a disruption of her life, God was unfolding a plan that she could not have imagined.

Of all the young women taken into the palace, it was Esther who found favor with the official in charge of the selection process. And this stranger's kindness toward her began a chain of favor that would position Esther to fulfill the plan God had for her life.

Favor changes everything. Favor will carry the faithful from obscurity to significance. Favor has nothing to do with luck or coincidence. It is an unseen and unthought-of divine intervention in the course of someone's life. When favor steps in, all the limitations fall off. Can you say, "I receive favor," and declare that your children are "surrounded with favor as a shield" (Ps. 5:12)?

Never forget—favor always has a purpose. Esther's favor

was not for her alone. God was positioning her to save thousands of innocent lives. I have to admit, however, that along the way she did receive some very nice benefits. The official who showed her favor gave her a private apartment in the king's palace. She was given beauty treatments, special food, and seven personal maids. Ladies, she was in spa heaven. I think I just heard someone say, "You go, girl!"

This was a very nice collateral blessing, but this was only the beginning of God's plan. Esther 2:15 tells us that she had favor with "everyone who saw her." Finally, when she went before the king, she found favor again (v. 17), and she was selected to be the new queen. But God still had bigger plans for her.

Esther's life as the new queen was going well. God's favor on her life was beyond all she could have ever imagined. And then Mordecai delivered some bad news: there was a plot to massacre all the Jews, and she alone was positioned to stop it. He told her that her meteoric rise to royalty was probably for just that moment. Esther now had to recognize that what God's favor had brought her was not nearly as important as why it had come.

Esther connected the dots and realized why she had become queen. She had been positioned to save the entire population of Jews living in Xerxes's kingdom. But time was of the essence. There was no time for typical palace protocol. She would have to approach the king without his formal invitation. To do this would put her very life at risk, but it had to be done.

Mordecai and Esther agreed to pray and fast for three days, and then she would approach the king. They did as agreed, and three days later Esther approached the king's throne. In a few minutes she would know whether she would live or die, and whether her people might be saved.

Once again, at the most critical moment, the favor of God was released on her life.

> When the king saw Queen Esther standing quietly out in the courtyard, she gained favor in his sight, so the king held out the golden scepter in his hand to Esther. Esther approached and touched the top of the scepter.
>
> —ESTHER 5:2, MEV

Favor on this day spared Esther's life. In the next verse we read that the king allowed her to make any request. So there she stood before the king with the invitation to ask him whatever she wanted. Only God could orchestrate something like that!

You probably know the rest of the story. Esther was able to save her people by uncovering the evil scheme intended to annihilate them. Instead of the Jewish people being killed, the man behind the plot ended up losing his life.

THE CHAIN OF FAVOR

I wanted to share Esther's story so you could see how the chain of favor operates. This is the concept I want you to have in mind as you pray for your children and declare God's favor over them. Your children must have divine favor to position them, promote them, protect them, and provide for them as they move through their school years and then on to adulthood.

Favor can show up at any moment and reverse every setback in your life or your child's life. In fact, God may be using your current setback to set you up to receive His favor. Favor can get you unstuck, get back what you lost while you were in that stuck place, and then propel you into your promise. This is the chain of favor God often works in our lives. He gives us favor to get out, get back, and get in.

We see this chain of favor in the account of Joseph. This was a young man with big dreams and big challenges. The son of Abraham's grandson Jacob, Joseph received a life dream from God, but his family rejected both him and the dream. In fact, the animosity of his older brothers reached such a level that they almost killed him but at the last minute decided to sell him as a slave instead.

Joseph was taken to Egypt and bought by Potiphar, one of Pharaoh's officials. We read that the Lord was with Joseph there and that he prospered despite his situation. Maybe your child has been abandoned by her father and you feel alone in raising her. Be encouraged. God is with you when others have rejected you. You and your child can prosper in the midst of circumstances that are less than ideal.

We see throughout Joseph's story that wherever he was, he always did the best he could with what he had, which is a practice that invites God's favor. But I'm sure he still had questions. Why did his family reject him? Why was he now a slave? How would he ever see the fulfillment of the dream God had given him? Joseph had to trust in God's goodness because those answers were a long time coming. Joseph's chain of favor had some very difficult links.

Just when his situation seemed to be improving, he faced a setback. Potiphar's wife had become infatuated with this handsome young Hebrew. Again and again she attempted to seduce him, and again and again Joseph refused her. Then one day in the anger resulting from his refusals, she falsely accused Joseph of trying to rape her. Of course, her husband believed her, and he threw Joseph in prison. But this was not just any prison—it was where the king's prisoners were confined. This was probably the worst prison in which to be incarcerated, but it proved to be the very best place for Joseph.

At this point it seemed that Joseph's life had literally hit rock bottom. He may have thought all his hopes and dreams would end there. That might have been true…if favor had not walked in. Genesis 39:21 alerts us to the fact that at the lowest point of Joseph's life, he again found favor: "But the LORD was with Joseph and showed him mercy and gave him favor in the sight of the keeper of the prison" (MEV).

To fulfill the purpose of God for him, Joseph had to connect with Pharaoh, and prison was the path that would take him there. This isn't the end of Joseph's story, but there is a profound truth right here that I hope you can see: you may not like who's driving the bus on your way to favor, but stay on board anyway. You don't want to get off one stop before favor gets on!

In prison, Joseph interpreted a dream for Pharaoh's former cupbearer, and the events unfolded just as Joseph revealed. The cupbearer was restored to his position before Pharaoh. When he was released from prison he forgot all about Joseph until two years later when Pharaoh had a dream no one could interpret. The cupbearer remembered Joseph, and in short order Joseph was standing before Pharaoh. Again God enabled Joseph to correctly interpret the dream, and Joseph was instantly released from prison and promoted to Egypt's second-in-command. Only Pharaoh had more authority than Joseph.

What a stunning turnaround! In twenty-four hours, Joseph's life was changed forever. How? Favor! Favor can take you from the prison to the palace in one giant step. Just don't forget that God gives favor for a purpose. Like Esther, Joseph was positioned to save thousands of lives, this time from a deadly famine.

You must believe that no matter how impossible your current season, God can release favor to *get you out*! But that's not all. While you were trapped in your prison season, you may have lost some things. Satan is the thief that comes "only to steal and kill and destroy" (John 10:10). But don't worry, favor can also bring the restoration of all that the enemy has stolen!

Because of God's favor, you can *get back* everything that has been taken or lost. This is exactly what God did for the Israelites after they had been enslaved in Egypt for four hundred years. God said, "I will make the Egyptians favorably disposed toward this people, so that when you leave you will not go empty-handed" (Exod. 3:21).

What did God mean exactly? Would they merely leave with their valuables? No, the reach of favor went much further than that. God said, "Every woman is to ask her neighbor and any woman living in her house for articles of silver and gold and for clothing [I'm sorry to interrupt here, but you know when a woman willingly hands over her clothes and jewelry, God is moving!], which you will put on your sons and daughters. And so you will plunder the Egyptians" (Exod. 3:22).

Plunder is a very strong word. It is used in reference to

warfare. When one army has defeated an opposing army, they plunder them. By force they take for themselves everything of value. *Plunder* is never used to describe a willing gift. The King James Version says the Israelites would "spoil" the Egyptians on that day. Plunder is the spoils of war.

When the Israelites were leaving Egypt, they only had to ask for their neighbors' clothing and jewelry. Yet the Bible makes it seem as though the Israelites plundered the Egyptians. Could this be an insight into spiritual warfare? When we win in the spiritual, we receive in the natural. It may not be clothes, jewelry, or money, but our prayer for favor will cause us to get back that which we never could have reclaimed in our own ability. The battle is the Lord's.

God gives us favor to *get back*. The Israelites had been slaves in Egypt for four hundred long years. After four centuries of lost wages, they had nothing with which to begin their journey to the Promised Land. But they had God's favor operating on their behalf. That's how in one day the wealth of the richest empire on the planet was transferred to a nation of slaves. And not one drop of blood was shed. Wealth lost after four hundred years of slavery was restored in one day. There is no parallel in human history.

Who could have imagined how God would get back what had been lost? When favor shows up, it can turn your greatest oppressor into your greatest benefactor. And remember, favor may appear in the most unusual circumstances from the most unexpected sources. Just because you cannot imagine it doesn't mean that God cannot do it.

This is restoration favor. You see, the biblical definition of restoration goes beyond that of Webster's dictionary. When we try to restore something, our goal is to bring it back as close to its original condition as possible. The restoration of an antique car or a piece of furniture may come to mind. Much time and elbow grease is invested to see how close we can bring the item to its former appearance and function.

When the Bible uses the term *restoration*, it is talking about restoration on an entirely different level. In biblical restoration, the person or situation is better than it was before. So when God's favor gets something back—restores it—it is better than, superior to, greater than even its original condition.

Take a moment here and think about your life in view of God's favor to get back. What has life stolen from you or your children? Turn that over to God right now. The people who have broken their promises or crushed your dreams are not your source. Let go of them. Forgive them. Stop trying to collect an old debt from a past relationship and believe God has the power to restore. We often keep trying to make things like they were when we should be moving forward to something better.

God's favor will not only get you out and get it back, favor will *get you in*. Our God always has purposes connected to His favor. The God who is able to get you out and get back what has been lost or stolen will not leave you at this point. This was all necessary to get you into your promised land so you can take hold of your dreams and fulfill every plan God has for you.

Here's what God says about favor to get in:

> For they did not take possession of the land by
> their own sword, nor did their own arm save them;

> but it was Your right hand, and Your arm, and the
> light of Your countenance, because You had favor
> on them.
> —Psalm 44:3, mev

God's plan for your life is not to release you from your past just so you can wander around in the wilderness. He brought you out and restored your losses to move you into His plan. Don't stop short. Don't settle for less than God's best for you or your child. God's favor can put you in possession of your greatest dream. Favor does not only give you a promise, it enables you to possess the promise.

God doesn't want you and your child to live lives of "halfway there." But your ability to step into God's best for your life will never be enough by itself. You need God to accomplish this, and this is how He will do it: His right hand, His arm, and His favor. You need God to go before you and make a way for you to step into your new season.

In Psalm 44:2, the verse just before the one quoted above, the Bible tells us that God drove out the nations, planted His people, and made them flourish: "With your hand you drove out the nations and planted our ancestors; you crushed the peoples and made our ancestors flourish." Let this verse remind you that God will *always* finish everything He starts. He won't bring you out of a situation and leave you hanging. His favor will get you out, get back what you have lost, and then get you into the place of your destiny.

An Appointment With Favor

The road to favor is not always smooth or easily understood. There will be moments when it seems like everything but favor is happening in your life. That's OK. You're in some pretty good company. Esther had these seasons and so did Joseph. They stayed on track by remaining faithful to God in every circumstance. As I said earlier, they did what they could where they were with what they had. Faith in your future will release patience in your present. Jesus endured the shame of the Cross by focusing on the joy that was set before Him (Heb. 12:2).

As you pray for favor to surround your child like a shield, you must be determined to remain faithful to God. You will never know how close you are to seeing His favor show up in your life or your child's. Psalm 102:13 reveals that favor has an appointed time to intersect our lives. It says, "You will arise and have compassion on Zion, for it is time to show favor to her; the appointed time has come."

Your favor is part of a divine assignment, and it will be released in your life in the perfect timing of God. Trust that He sees and knows that which is beyond your understanding. What if your favor to get in is on God's timetable for tomorrow? You could be on the very eve of a breakthrough of favor. Don't give up now. Take a firmer grip and pray one more day.

Think of the young Virgin Mary. When the angel visited her in Nazareth and revealed God's purpose for her life, she was understandably overwhelmed. The Bible declares in Luke 1 that she would give birth to the Son of God because she had received favor. But I'm sure there were moments over the next nine months when she may not have felt so highly favored.

If Joseph, her fiancé, required an angelic visitation before he could believe her, can you imagine the reaction she received from everyone else who knew her? Think about it. She was a young girl, engaged but not married, walking around pregnant. It would take quite a bit of faith to see that as a favored position.

Then the Roman emperor Caesar decreed that a census must be taken of the entire Roman world, and everyone had to return to their hometown to register. That's not quite what a pregnant woman in her last trimester wants to hear. The little expectant girl would now be forced to ride a donkey from Nazareth to Bethlehem—not an easy, comfortable trip.

But God had not forgotten about Mary. God caused the entire Roman world to take a census because Mary had an appointment with favor. She would never have taken that journey to Bethlehem without Caesar's decree. And had she not taken that journey, the promised Messiah would not have been born in Bethlehem as prophecy foretold (Mic. 5:2).

That fact didn't make Mary's journey any easier. When she and Joseph finally arrived in Bethlehem, they were met by a throng of others coming to register. You probably know what else they discovered—no room available anywhere. Reluctantly Joseph had to accept his only option and take a very pregnant Mary to a stable to try to get some rest.

Mary may not have fully realized what was about to happen, but we know the greatest gift that God has ever given us was about to be born. Time would forever be divided in two: the period before His coming and the one after it. The world changed the day Jesus was born. Salvation had come to the world. Hope and grace had come. His was and will always be the most important birth of all the billions that have ever and will ever take place on planet Earth.

But just before this wonderful event took place, Mary may have had her toughest day ever. Think of the previous twenty-four hours of her life. A young woman ready to give birth any day spent hours riding a donkey of all things. Then, exhausted and uncomfortable, she was told there was nowhere safe and clean to lie down and rest. Can you imagine her thoughts as she stepped into that stable? The animals, the smells, the discomfort.

The eve of favor—the favor God was sending to all of us—was extremely difficult for Mary. But the story didn't end there. Weary from travel and trying to get comfortable in a stable, she went into labor. Unbelievable! No doctors or helpful nurses. Just a few disinterested donkeys, cattle, and maybe a horse or two. The day before God's favor would be released in the earth was probably not what Mary envisioned it would be.

Maybe yours won't be either. As you can see, it is sometimes difficult to recognize how close you are to your appointment with God's favor. The greatest labor pains come just before the birth, and the greatest joy comes just after it. Mary's pain gave way to the greatest promise mankind would ever receive, and God has a purpose for your pain too. Hang in there.

Before I close this chapter, I want to draw your attention to a few qualities evident in Mary's life. As I said before, divine favor cannot be earned, but I believe these traits positioned her to receive God's favor.

The Bible tells us that Mary was a virgin. When the angel told her she would conceive by God's Spirit, her response was,

"I am the servant of the Lord. May it be unto me according to your word" (Luke 1:38, MEV). In other words, she told God, "I'm Your servant; Your will be done." Here we see that Mary positioned herself to receive favor by living a life of holiness, and by trusting and submitting to God's will even when it didn't make sense to her.

As you intercede that God's favor will rest on your children, pray also that they will live pure, godly lives and be faithful to God's will, whether they understand it or not. But don't stop there. Teach them the importance of being obedient to God, honoring Him with their lifestyle, and doing the best they can with what they have. Then live that kind of life before them. This will position them—and you—to receive God's favor to get out, get back, and get in.

Now that you understand how divine favor works, I'm sure you want to see this blessing released in your children's lives. I know I do. I believe you're ready to pray, so let's do this. Let the following prayer serve as a guide as you intercede for God's favor to rest on your children.

> *Father, in Jesus's name, I decree that favor will be released in my child's life today. I declare that my child will honor You with his life, and that he will trust You and submit to Your will.*
>
> *In Jesus's name, I declare that my child will have favor with God and man. I thank You that favor now surrounds my child as a shield. He will have favor with every teacher in every class. My child will have favor with each principal and the administration of his school. He will have favor with every employee and volunteer at his school.*

> *My child will have favor with each and every*
> *student.*
>
> *This favor will position my child for promotion*
> *and protection. Your favor will have him at the*
> *right place at the right time. Your favor will give*
> *my child everything he needs so that everything*
> *my child puts his hand to will prosper. Thank You*
> *for this precious blessing, in Jesus's name, amen.*

You have one fortunate child to be prayed over in such a powerful, biblical fashion. We have one final lesson to learn from Daniel's amazing life, and it's a good one. This prayer principle will follow our children throughout their lives and cause them to rise above the status quo. I know you can't wait to learn this one, so let's go.

Chapter 7

PRAYER PRINCIPLE #5:
SUPERNATURAL PROMOTION
AND INFLUENCE

At the end of the time set by the king to bring them into his service, the chief official presented them to Nebuchadnezzar. The king talked with them, and he found none equal to Daniel, Hananiah, Mishael and Azariah; so they entered the king's service. In every matter of wisdom and understanding about which the king questioned them, he found them ten times better than all the magicians and enchanters in his whole kingdom.

—DANIEL 1:18–20

THERE ARE TWO phrases in the verses quoted at the opening of this chapter that I want you to notice. First, the passage says there were "none equal" to the four Hebrew boys. Next, it says they were "ten times better than all." I'm sure that these four were intelligent and studious, but that alone could not explain what we read here. Your children must study and apply themselves to their classwork if they are to develop. God cannot bless effort that is never taken. But when we do what we can, God will do what we cannot.

None equal to them? Ten times better than all? That is supernatural promotion. That level of excellence comes only from the hand of God to those who have "resolved" to serve the Lord. And these kinds of results come only as answers to prayer.

As we've studied the principles in the Daniel Prayer, we've prayed for our children's physical health and safety, their educational development and excellence, that they would come into a personal relationship with Jesus Christ and resolve to serve Him, and that God's favor would rest on their lives. Those prayer focuses are powerful and far reaching, but God wants to do more in your child's life. After covering all of those areas, we can then pray that God's plan for our children will be realized—that they will walk in supernatural promotion and influence.

This is not a selfish, narrow prayer. This fifth and final component of the Daniel Prayer is for our children, yet it is bigger than our children. You see, every promotion God gives comes as a platform to influence others for Christ.

Life is not just about what I can get for me and mine. Real life is about fulfilling God's will and making a difference. It's about influence. It's about using the gifts and talents God has given us to make our world a better place.

In his book *Made to Count*, author Bob Reccord discusses a survey that was taken across the United States. The poll asked only one question, "What's your greatest fear?" What do you think was the number one answer? Financial collapse, war, terrorism, Ebola? Out of a litany of possible responses, the most common answer by far was the fear of dying without having made a significant difference.[1]

I was surprised by the top answer initially, yet as I reflected on it, it made perfect sense. God put deep within every human being a yearning to know and walk with Him. When Adam and Eve longed to know God and walked closely with Him, they lived in the peace of a perfect, productive garden. But when disobedience caused them to hide from God rather than walk with Him, everything shifted downward. They lost their relationship with God, the authority God had given them to rule, and their sense of purpose because they were removed from the garden they had been commissioned to steward.

Still today mankind longs for the intimacy with God that Adam and Eve lost in the garden, but many have no idea what they're desiring or how to satisfy it. The great evangelist Billy Graham explains that this deep yearning to know God is a result of a God-shaped vacuum in our hearts. When our children (or anyone else for that matter) accept Christ as their Savior, that God-shaped void is filled. The pieces of the puzzle fall into place, and their lives come into order. Once they know Christ, He restores their sense of purpose, which is to make Him known through their unique talents and gifts. This is why we were all put on this planet.

Our children have a God-given desire to know the Lord personally. As this desire is satisfied and they develop in their walk with God, He will show them how to fulfill their need to make a difference. Then God will promote them so they can use the resources and opportunities He gives them to make Him known to those within their sphere of influence.

This final prayer focus of the Daniel Prayer empowers our children to live out this truth and have kingdom influence. It prepares them to recognize where their promotion comes from and how to use their blessings, favor, and influence to honor God.

We want our children's lives to be fulfilling and impactful.

When we pray for supernatural promotion and influence, we are praying that they will live at a much higher level of success. Too many people think success means getting all you can, canning what you get, and sitting on the can! But that is not true success.

We make a living with what we earn, but we make a life with what we give. Life is God's gift to us, but what we choose to do with our life is our gift to Him. To live out these truths is what it means to experience God's kind of influence.

The Bible tells us, "Whatever you do, work at it with all your heart, as working for the Lord, not for human masters, since you know that you will receive an inheritance from the Lord as a reward. It is the Lord Christ you are serving" (Col. 3:23–24). This is how those who understand true success choose to live.

When our children live to have God's kind of influence, they will do as Romans 12:1–2 says. They will offer themselves as living sacrifices to God, holy and pleasing to Him. They will not conform to the pattern of this world, but they will be transformed by the renewing of their minds. They will be able to test and approve what is God's good, pleasing, and perfect will. Isn't this the level at which you want your child to live?

NONE EQUAL

Remember what we are praying for our children or grandchildren: that none will be equal to them and that in every matter of wisdom and understanding they will be ten times better than all. That may seem lofty to you, but I encourage you: don't undersell your children or God as you pray for them. If you have a hard time believing that there would be none equal to your children, just pray that part of the Daniel Prayer until God gives you the faith to believe He will do it. These are not secondhand phrases to be mindlessly spoken. They are strong, determined declarations of faith.

It's important to understand this declaration that there would be "none equal" and they would be "ten times better than all" is for every child. Notice again with me exactly what the passage says about Daniel and his friends: "In every matter of wisdom and understanding about which the king questioned them, he found them ten times better than all the magicians and enchanters in his whole kingdom" (Dan. 1:20). Daniel and his friends weren't ten times better than all the fishermen in the kingdom, and they weren't questioned in every matter of bread making or stonemasonry. God caused them to excel in the areas in which He had gifted them and called them to influence.

Each child has unique abilities and potential. Each one has a rich capacity to learn. This prayer meets them where they are and releases them to be their very best.

Your child may be in a gifted student track. Wonderful. Declare by faith in God that there will be none equal to him and that he will be ten times better than all so he will be promoted and thereby positioned for godly influence in that sphere.

Your child may be in a remedial class or two. Thank God for this opportunity for special attention. But do not accept less than God's best for your child. Pray this prayer for your child right where she is. Pray that there will be none equal to her in that class and that she will be found to be ten times better than all. This prayer is really not about comparing your child to others. It's about blessing your child to do her best.

You may have a special-needs child whose capacity to

learn is different from another child's. God's blessing and favor is not doled out in proportion to IQ or aptitude test scores. Celebrate this child and the setting in which he can experience promotion and influence. Pray that there would be none equal in your child's class or group and that your child would be ten times better than all. God can use your child's excellence as a testimony of His power.

We never know whom God will greatly use or how He will choose to do so. Only God knows each child's purpose and potential. Our role as parents, grandparents, or guardians is to faithfully pray for our children, love them, and encourage them.

As we pray for God to bless and develop our children for supernatural promotion, we will begin to see them through God's eyes. This may force us to reevaluate our perceptions of our children, and we may need to change our thinking and begin to agree with God's purpose for them. If we let Him, God will help us to see our children as unique individuals and be patient with them as they develop.

When you hear the name Albert Einstein you immediately think of genius. Yet in the many biographies written about his life, it is clear that he started rather slowly. This brilliant physicist had to find his own educational path and pace. Much has been written about his delayed speech development. However, Einstein began writing between the ages of two and three; he would practice sentences nonverbally before he would say them aloud. That was just his way of processing. Intellectually, he was fine.[2]

Einstein admitted that he had difficulty with memorization. He once wrote of test taking, "I would feel under such strain that I felt, rather than going to take a test that instead, I was walking to the guillotine." He also said one of his teachers once told him he "would never be able to do anything that would make any sense in this life."[3]

He had some challenges, yes. He may have been a bit of a "late bloomer." He seemed to learn and process a little differently. But as you may have heard, it's not how you start that matters most, it's how you finish. Einstein's life was a clear testament to this.

So do not categorize or label your child too quickly. Only God knows all that he or she can become. This is why praying for your child's promotion and influence is imperative. Your faithful prayers for your child connect heaven and earth. They connect what you can see with what only God can see. Your intercession takes the hand of your child and connects it to the hand of our mighty God. In that connection what is impossible with man becomes possible with God.

DECLARE BOLDLY

I want to commend you for reading a book devoted to praying for your children. God is pleased with you. You have His attention and His resources focused in your direction. Don't be intimidated to bring big prayers before Him. The Bible tells us, "For the eyes of the LORD run to and fro throughout the whole earth, to show Himself strong on behalf of those whose heart is loyal to Him" (2 Chron. 16:9, NKJV).

To pray that there will be "none equal" to your child and that she will be "ten times better than all" requires that you occupy a bold position in intercession. This is not a pleading prayer; it's a proclaiming prayer. It is a prayer of declaration.

You could say that you are not only praying, you are prophesying what God has said in His Word. Under the anointing of the Holy Spirit you are "speaking forth" the Word of God. You don't have to be a prophet to speak forth God's will and Word by the empowerment of the Holy Spirit. Every believer is qualified to do this. Your biblically based prayer, anointed by the Holy Spirit, is supernaturally effective.

In chapter 2 we discussed how Joshua led the Israelites to take possession of the Promised Land. As they went kingdom by kingdom and city by city routing out the residents and occupying the land, they opened the door for the next generation to live in the land in peace. The parents fought battles and cleared out enemies so their children could possess everything God had promised.

In a similar way, as you pray this Daniel Prayer you are clearing the way for your children to walk in their destiny by routing out the spiritual forces that would oppose them. The Bible tells us, "Finally, be strong in the Lord and in his mighty power. Put on the full armor of God, so that you can take your stand against the devil's schemes. For our struggle is not against flesh and blood, but against the rulers, against the authorities, against the powers of this dark world and against the spiritual forces of evil in the heavenly realms" (Eph. 6:10–12). We are in a battle for our children's future, and the evil forces we contend with will be defeated only through the partnership of God's Word and His Spirit being released through prayer.

I will never forget hearing evangelist Reinhard Bonnke tell of a pivotal encounter he had with God when he was still a young missionary. He was serving in Africa at the time, but the awe-inspiring evangelistic ministry he would later become known for had not yet begun. On this occasion he had secured a prominent evangelist to conduct a large crusade. On the day the much-anticipated crusade was to begin, the evangelist told Brother Bonnke that he would not be able to speak in the services.

Brother Bonnke was devastated. What would he do now? The crowd was already waiting. It was too late to cancel. Surely he would never be trusted to lead such an effort again. As he began to desperately pray, God spoke to him: "Reinhard, My word in your mouth is as powerful as My word in My mouth"! God then told him that he would be the crusade speaker. Since then millions have been saved through Brother Bonnke's crusades throughout Africa. Each time he speaks in those events, God is confirming this word yet again.[4]

God was teaching Brother Bonnke about the power of declaring His Word, but the lesson was not for him alone. God's Word is also powerful in our mouths. Through our prayers, we can speak His Word into any situation. And when the anointed Word of God is released, there is nothing that can stand against its force.

The Bible says, "So is my word that goes out from my mouth: It will not return to me empty, but will accomplish what I desire and achieve the purpose for which I sent it" (Isa. 55:11). That is an incredible promise! Keep that at the forefront of your mind as you declare God's will, which is His Word, over your child. Boldly declare that your child will be excellent and have supernatural promotion and influence!

The prophet Ezekiel had an experience with God that reminds me of Reinhard Bonnke's crisis encounter. In Ezekiel 37, the prophet was confronted with a scenario that seemed impossible. He was taken by God and set in the middle of a valley. But this was not just any valley. It was a valley where a vast army had died in battle. Evidently, the defeat had been so complete and the body count so high that no one had been buried. The defeat had been so devastating that those who survived just never returned. I imagine they walked away and tried to forget.

This place of defeat and intimidation had been left unchallenged for so long that the bones were now very dry and scattered. Even though Ezekiel was a prophet, when God asked him if those bones could live again, he could not answer. The best he could muster was, "Sovereign LORD, you alone know" (Ezek. 37:3). The prophet was stuck. The situation seemed impossible. Even he could not imagine how God could do something of that scope. One man returning to life was one thing, but thousands? Ezekiel just did not know.

Have you ever faced an impossible situation in your child's life? Have you ever gone through something so challenging you weren't sure what to pray—or even if you could pray? Let me tell you, God has given you a key to create possibility in the valley of your impossibility. It is so simple yet so profound: speak forth His Word.

Reinhard Bonnke was not sure what to do when faced with an impossible situation. So was Ezekiel, and you may be too. But God's response is constant: "Say what I have said. Speak that which has come from My mouth, and the limits will simply dissolve."

God told Ezekiel what to say. He told him to prophesy to the bones, and when he did they came together. Ezekiel then was told to prophesy that breath would return to them—and it did. A once dead and defeated army stood to their feet. Ezekiel would never be the same and neither would those resurrected soldiers.

I pray that this book will stretch your faith and cause you to have an encounter with God that will completely transform how you pray for your dear children. I believe that again today God would be pleased to raise up an army of Spirit-filled students to change our world, just as He did in Daniel's day. School may be tough at times, and your children may go through difficult seasons. Don't be discouraged. Your problem is no match for God. No matter what your children or your family may be facing, it's not as hopeless as a valley of dry bones.

THE POWER OF A PARENT'S BLESSING

The Daniel Prayer is more than just words we speak each day. Each time we pray it over our children, we are declaring a blessing over them.

The opportunity to bless our children is a priceless gift God has given parents, grandparents, and guardians. A blessing is the impartation of the supernatural power of God into a human life through words spoken by God's delegated authority. As a parent you are the delegated authority God wants to use to impart His blessing into your child—a blessing that will empower him to fulfill God's assignment for his life.

God set the precedent for blessing His children in the very first chapter of Scripture. After God created Adam and Eve in His image and likeness, the first thing He did was to immediately bless them (Gen. 1:28). Before they could earn it, God willingly gave them His blessing.

This blessing was not just a random expression of well wishing. It carried the spiritual power that would equip Adam and Eve to become God's representatives on earth. This unearned gift of blessing empowered them to manage everything God had created and thus fulfill their destiny.

But the blessing does more than deliver God's power. It will also repel every curse or evil plan of the enemy. God's Word says, "See, I have received a commandment to bless, and He has blessed, and I cannot reverse it" (Num. 23:20, MEV). God also told the prophet not to even attempt to curse the Israelites "because they are blessed" (Num. 22:12, MEV).

The blessing also carries the power to overcome every natural hindrance to God's plan for someone's life. In Genesis 48, when Israel was near death, Joseph brought his two sons to him to receive their grandfather's blessing. Joseph was concerned that his father's failing eyesight might cause confusion, so Joseph planned to take his father's right hand and place it on the head of his elder son, Manasseh, as was the custom. Traditionally the older son received the greater blessing.

But Israel placed his right hand on Ephraim's head, even though he was the younger son. Notice here the Bible says that "crossing his arms" (Gen. 48:14), Israel put his left hand on Manasseh's head and his right hand on Ephraim's.

There is such a powerful message imbedded in that act. You see, when Israel made a cross with his arms, he broke tradition to bless the younger son. That's what Jesus did on the cross for you, me, and our children. On the cross, Jesus took the curse of sin upon Himself so that we could be blessed (Gal. 3:13–14). We did not deserve to be blessed; Christ did. But the Cross brought blessing to the ones who least deserved it.

When your child is blessed, God moves him into a place where he will receive unearned and undeserved benefits. The blessing of God is a million times better than being born with a silver spoon in your mouth. And you don't need special permission to give your child this gift. The Cross has authorized you to speak the blessing of God to your child. When you do, there is no family history or power of hell that can undo the power of God's blessing on your child's life.

There is nothing magical about a blessing. The power of blessing comes from the power of God's Word. But a blessing must be spoken. This is because your children need to hear the words you are declaring. For children to hear their parents bless and affirm them is as nourishing as water is to a plant. These Holy Spirit–empowered words will shape your children's identity and fill them with hope and courage for the future.

In addition to praying the Daniel Prayer over your child, periodically let your children hear you praying this over them. Adjust the phrasing so that you speak the prayer as a blessing over your child. This prayer is not a meditation; it is a declaration. It is a prophetic utterance that carries God's creative power. Words have life and power. The Bible tells us, "The tongue has the power of life and death, and those who love it will eat its fruit" (Prov. 18:21). God created the universe by His spoken word. And when you speak His Word in prayer, it will release His power to establish your child.

Scripture says, "By faith Isaac blessed Jacob and Esau in regard to their future" (Heb. 11:20). By faith, boldly declare

God's blessing on your children by praying for their physical health and safety, for their educational development and excellence, that they would resolve to serve the Lord, that they would have divine favor, and that they would receive supernatural promotion and influence. When you do, God will impart His supernatural power into their lives.

I believe you have been well equipped to pray the Daniel Prayer for Parents with great faith and understanding. These prayer principles are so mighty, and the effect of praying them is so far reaching. I have so much holy expectation and anticipation to see the results in your child's life.

I am in agreement with you as you pray this final aspect of the Daniel Prayer for your child. You can alter it as you feel led, but let it serve as a guide for proclaiming blessing and supernatural promotion over your child.

> *Father, I come to You right now in Jesus's name. I pray that when my child takes a test or exam, or when he is considered for special opportunities, that like Daniel and his friends he will be found ten times better than all, and that none will be found equal.*
>
> *I pray that my child will retain and recall everything he has studied. Because of Your favor, my child will be promoted and recognized and have great influence for Christ. I declare that my child is blessed with Your supernatural power to fulfill his destiny. [Insert your child's name] is blessed and no curse can come to rest upon him. Again, this I pray in Jesus's name. Amen.*

Wow! I can sense a holy boldness rising up as parents declare that their children will be blessed and not cursed, and that they will receive supernatural promotion to become a great influence for Christ. Please don't ever underestimate the power of prayer. Our prayers for our children are shaping the destiny of a generation.

Prayer works—and the Daniel Prayer works. As we close out this book, I want to put all the pieces together for you and show you the difference this prayer can make in a child's life.

Conclusion

IT WORKS!

The prayer of a righteous person is powerful and effective.

—James 5:16

Now that we've covered the principles at the center of the Daniel Prayer for Parents, it's time to put it all together. Before you receive the entire prayer that I shared with my congregation on that Back to School Sunday, I want you to understand the divine power at the root of each part of the prayer. Only by understanding the divine truths that underscore each aspect of the prayer can you pray these principles with faith and expectancy.

As I've said before, this is not meant to be prayed by rote. It is to serve as a guide for you to alter as the Holy Spirit leads you and as your child's needs change. Let this prayer come alive in your heart and transform your intercession for your child.

THE DANIEL PRAYER FOR PARENTS

Father, I come to You today in the name of Jesus. I am here to declare favor and blessing over my child.

I pray that today and every day my child will walk in divine health and healing. I declare that no sickness or disease will enter his body. No accident, harm, wound, or assault can touch him. I pray that by the stripes of Jesus he is healed today. I thank

You that You have provided healing as the children's daily bread (Matt. 15:22–26).

Just as Daniel and his friends showed aptitude for every kind of learning, and were well informed and quick to understand, I pray today and every day that my child will develop academically and have educational excellence. I pray that he will have divine wisdom and understanding for every subject. I declare that he will comprehend and retain the material presented in every class. I declare that my child will be attentive, courteous, and diligent to study. Nothing will be too difficult for him.

Father, just as Daniel resolved to serve You, I pray this day that my child will come into a personal relationship with Jesus as his Savior. I declare that my child will be born again and be filled with Your Holy Spirit. I thank You that as a young believer he will resolve and determine to serve the Lord. As Daniel refused to eat with others at the king's table, so will my child refuse to compromise and give in to peer pressure. He will be an influencer and not the influenced.

I declare that today and every day my child is surrounded with favor like a shield. He will receive favor from every teacher and principal. He will be favored by every employee and volunteer at his school. He will have favor with every student and receive the blessings that only favor could provide.

And just as there were none equal to Daniel and his friends and they were ten times better than all, I decree and declare today and every day

*that my child has a supernatural ability to learn.
When he takes tests and exams, he will retain and
recall all he has learned. As a result of God's grace
he will be recognized and promoted, for there is
none equal to my child, and he is ten times better
than all. This blessing will—and has—positioned
my child for promotion, and he will have the
wisdom to use this as a platform to bring influence for Christ.*

*Thank You for my child. Today I boldly speak
each one of these blessings over him. I declare that
my child is blessed and highly favored, in Jesus's
name. Amen.*

As you pray this daily over your children, its impact
and effectiveness will begin to grow. The steady deposit of
this prayer is like the upward push of a mighty geyser of
blessing and favor. It will erupt in an unstoppable torrent
of promotion and influence in your child's life. Your child
will be enabled by God's response to your prayers to live in
the center of His will. You are literally praying your son or
daughter into a life that only God could have designed.

The focus, the passion, and the purpose of this prayer is
for God's highest purpose to be realized in your child's life.
This is not a prayer spoken by someone groveling before an
uninterested God. You are humbly yet boldly in the authority
of Christ declaring your child's destiny.

You have read testimonies throughout this book of how
God answered the prayers of praying parents. By way of
closing, I want to share one last testimony sent to me from

a member of our church. It is a powerful example of how praying the Daniel Prayer can impact a child's life.

———— • ————

I've never been a morning person. My husband always bounds out of bed, heading straight to our garden to pray. But my body and brain have always fought against morning's first light.

After Pastor Sawyer declared the Daniel Prayer over all the students, he admonished us parents and grandparents to pray it daily. So I strategically slipped a copy of the prayer next to my coffeepot so I would see it first thing each morning. But in those early days, I essentially recited it as I prayed for my granddaughter.

I couldn't see it initially, but in the depths of my heart, where only God could see, I had tremendous pride. My granddaughter was already extremely smart. She had favor and associated with godly friends. She was dedicated to the Lord as a baby, and we always believed she would do something great for God. I prayed the Daniel Prayer, but I believed it was already being answered.

My granddaughter was a model child. When we put her in the nursery as a baby, her number never flashed for us to pick her up. As she got older, she was selected to attend a magnet elementary school made up primarily of high achievers with few behavioral problems. She made excellent grades and received school awards. But her greatest achievement was sharing Jesus with another little girl. The child had never been told about Him before, and that precious little one accepted Christ as her Savior after my granddaughter shared the gospel with her!

We couldn't have been prouder. Everything was great, except that she was sometimes hyper. Just a little anxious, nothing to worry about. But it was enough for others to be concerned, and she was eventually diagnosed with attention deficit hyperactivity disorder (ADHD). We didn't let the diagnosis change our expectations for her in any way. We knew she was still a high achiever. We knew she would fulfill a great call of God on her life.

Then came sixth grade. Middle school was a whole new world, with new kids and new rules. My granddaughter seemed to be a fish out of water; it was hard for her to "go with the flow." That year her parents separated, and the family dog died. Suddenly the girl who had danced since she was two years old wanted to sit out. And when she was in children's church, her number came up.

So now in the mornings, I'd make my way to the coffeepot, bleary eyed, and then into the garden, where I began to pray, not recite, the Daniel Prayer. My husband, of course, was already there, praying for our granddaughter as well. My daughter also prayed the Daniel Prayer over her daughter. And we can all tell you, it works.

I would begin by praying, "Lord, I thank You for my grandchild. I declare this prayer over her as she goes to school today. She will have Your favor and blessing, even in difficult places, just as You gave Daniel in Babylon."

My granddaughter certainly was in a difficult place. One afternoon after school she told me, "God has told me He has something for me to do. It has something to do with my talent. I don't know what." I told her, "Be prepared, and at the right time He will reveal it." He did during Calvary Assembly's 2013

Christmas production. Another dancer was unable to participate, so my granddaughter was asked to fill in. She glided effortlessly across the floor, truly praising her Lord and Savior in dance. I saw joy return to her eyes and her heart.

Although this happened at church, not at school, I knew this was the Lord's favor and blessing working in my granddaughter's life. He gave her back her joy. Her praise began to tear down the walls, the difficult places in her life, just as praise brought down the walls of Jericho. I knew this was a sign of God's favor!

And signs of His favor kept coming. I had been concerned that my darling girl might not be chosen for her school's chorale ensemble, a group she desired with all her heart to be a part of. Admittance required auditioning. But her faith was great, and we were overjoyed when we received the good news that she was accepted. As she began to delight in the Lord, He was giving her the desires of her heart, just as Psalm 37:4 says.

Then we saw God's favor yet again. Science has always been my granddaughter's favorite subject. But in 2014 she told me that it was difficult for her to hear the teacher because so many children were talking out of turn in the classroom. Despite this difficulty, she maintained an A-plus average. I believe that was God's favor again!

As I continued to go through the Daniel Prayer, I would pray, "I declare in Jesus's name that my granddaughter is physically well and standing strong. No sickness, disease, accident, or injury will touch her. She will walk in divine health."

My granddaughter's physical health has always been good, though her doctor still says she has ADHD. Despite this diagnosis, she is doing very well academically and has had no behavioral problems. We are continuing to stand in faith and declare that she will walk in divine health in every aspect of her life. God's Word says, "I will bring health and healing to it; I will heal my people and will let them enjoy abundant peace and security" (Jer. 33:6). We are holding on to that promise for my granddaughter—that she will be physically well, standing strong, with no accidents or injuries.

Next in my Daniel Prayer, I would say, "I declare in Jesus's name that my granddaughter has the aptitude and ability to quickly understand, comprehend, and retain the knowledge of every subject she will be taught."

As I said, my granddaughter has always been a good student, but I still believe her academic success is an answer to prayer. In her final report card last year, she received five A-pluses and two As. So far this year, she has maintained these grades even in her two honors classes. And in history, one of her least-favorite subjects, she has maintained an A-plus average. I believe God is answering our prayers for her by giving her aptitude, ability, comprehension, retention, and favor!

As I continued the Daniel Prayer, I would declare, "My granddaughter will resolve, choose, and determine not to defile herself by eating or participating at the table of peer pressure."

My granddaughter, like most, desires to fit in, to be popular and liked by her peers. To achieve this in the natural, many girls choose to look a certain way, act a certain way, talk a certain way, and so on. Refusing to conform to the group's standards usually means exclusion and sometimes persecution. To my knowledge, my granddaughter has not yet faced the pressure to drink alcohol or do drugs. But I know she has been tempted to compromise her values to fit in.

Some friends of hers decided to reject a new girl at school because she somehow didn't measure up. My granddaughter refused to join in with them. She did not defile herself by participating at the tables of peer pressure! I know this is just the beginning of the pressures young people face in school today. But I believe that refusing to compromise to fit in with the popular crowd will help my granddaughter refuse to compromise when faced with even more serious temptations. It's as Jesus said, "Whoever can be trusted with very little can also be trusted with much, and whoever is dishonest with very little will also be dishonest with much" (Luke 16:10).

When I'd prayed the Daniel Prayer over my granddaughter, I prayed that she would choose to feed on God's Word and fellowship with the godly. And I'd declare that she would have favor with every principal, teacher, coach, and school official.

She does feed on God's Word, having been served it since she was a baby. And most of her school friends and their families attend church, though I cannot testify as to their godliness. Since she has moved into the teen ministry at church, she has been eager to participate and develop godly relationships with other students in the ministry. As I mentioned before, the little evangelist led a child to Jesus in elementary school, and she has recently invited other students at her school to attend church with her. One girl is now attending.

Her progress reports consistently contain comments from teachers that she is a good student and has a good attitude. I believe this is an answer to prayer.

As I near the close of my prayer for my granddaughter, I'd make a bold declaration. I would say: "I declare that because of God's favor and blessing and because of this prayer and her resolve to follow God, when she is tested, questioned, or considered, none will be found equal to her. In every matter of wisdom and understanding, she will be found ten times better than all!"

That's a bold prayer, but I can attest that God answers it in unique ways for each child. While I was writing this testimony, my granddaughter told me that the principal called her and some other students to the auditorium. She was afraid she had done something wrong. She had indeed done something—scored in the top 5 percent nationwide on an ACT Aspire test that qualified her to participate in Duke University's talent identification program. She, a seventh grader, was invited to take the ACT or SAT college entrance exam after which Duke University would provide a network of academic opportunities and resources based on her performance.

God used her academic excellence to set her apart from her peers. He might use another area of giftedness in another child, but I believe that in whatever way He chooses, He will answer our prayers for promotion and influence, and that when they are tested, questioned, or considered, He will cause our children to be found ten times better than all.

The Daniel Prayer works. I've learned to get up in the morning to meet God in the garden, because He truly does answer our prayers for our children.[1]

———◆———

Are you excited yet? Do you have a sense of expectation that God wants to take your prayers for your children to a whole new level?

It is no coincidence that you have found and read this book. I'm convinced that this is a divine appointment for you and your children. As you begin to pray the anointed truths of this prayer, great fruit will begin to be borne and manifested in the lives of your children.

I am in agreement with you each day as I declare the Daniel Prayer over my family. I believe this prayer is part of a movement that has been released from the very heart of God. Our children and our children's children will walk in divine health and healing. They will show aptitude for every kind of learning and be quick to understand every subject. They will have a genuine personal relationship with Jesus Christ and the resolve to serve Him in every situation. Divine favor will mark their lives and surround them like a shield. They will excel on every test and be recognized and promoted for there will be none like them, for by God's grace they will be ten times better than all. And they will have the wisdom of God to use this platform of promotion to bring influence for Christ!

As we remain faithful in prayer, together we can raise and release generations that will live at the highest level and give all the glory to God. Let the journey begin!

Appendix

THE DANIEL PRAYER
FOR PARENTS

Father, I come to You today in the name of Jesus. I am here to declare favor and blessing over my child.

I pray that today and every day my child will walk in divine health and healing. I declare that no sickness or disease will enter his body. No accident, harm, wound, or assault can touch him. I pray that by the stripes of Jesus he is healed today. I thank You that You have provided healing as the children's daily bread (Matt. 15:22–26).

Just as Daniel and his friends showed aptitude for every kind of learning, and were well informed and quick to understand, I pray today and every day that my child will develop academically and have educational excellence. I pray that he will have divine wisdom and understanding for every subject. I declare that he will comprehend and retain the material presented in every class. I declare that my child will be attentive, courteous, and diligent to study. Nothing will be too difficult for him.

Father, just as Daniel resolved to serve You, I pray this day that my child will come into a personal relationship with Jesus as his Savior. I declare that my child will be born again and be filled with Your Holy Spirit. I thank You that as a young believer he will resolve and determine to serve the Lord. As Daniel refused to eat with others at the king's table, so will my child refuse to compromise and give in to peer pressure. He will be an influencer and not the influenced.

I declare that today and every day my child is surrounded with favor like a shield. He will receive favor from every teacher and principal. He will be favored by every employee and volunteer at his school. He will have favor with every student and receive the blessings that only favor could provide.

And just as there were none equal to Daniel and his friends and they were ten times better than all, I decree and declare today and every day that my child has a supernatural ability to learn. When he takes tests and exams he will retain and recall all he has learned. I declare that there is none equal to my child and he is ten times better than all. This blessing will—and has—positioned my child for promotion and influence.

Thank You for my child. Today I boldly speak each one of these blessings over him. I declare that my child is blessed and highly favored, in Jesus's name. Amen.

NOTES

CHAPTER 1
YOUR PRAYERS MAKE A DIFFERENCE

1. Myles Munroe, *Understanding the Purpose and Power of Woman* (New Kensington, PA: Whitaker Image, 2001).

2. Definitions of Hebrew and Babylonian names drawn from Strong's Concordance with Hebrew and Greek Lexicon, found at www.eliyah.com/lexicon.html, and developed based on the author's study of original Hebrew root words and their uses in various Bible translations.

3. The Barna Group, "Five Myths About Young Adult Church Dropouts," November 16, 2011, accessed February 10, 2015, https://www.barna.org/teens-next-gen-articles/534-five -myths-about-young-adult-church-dropouts.

CHAPTER 2
BRINGING HEAVEN TO EARTH

1. Dutch Sheets, *Authority in Prayer* (Grand Rapids, MI: Bethany House, 2006), 20.

2. Ibid.

3. The NAS New Testament Greek Lexicon, s.v. "*Deesis*," http://www.biblestudytools.com/lexicons/greek/nas/deesis.html.

4. Desmond T. Evans, *Devotional Living* (N.p.: n.d.).

5. Jack Hayford, *Prayer Is Invading the Impossible* (South Plainfield, NJ: Logos International, 1977), 136.

6. Paul E. Billheimer, as quoted in Adam Stadtmiller, *Praying for Your Elephant* (Colorado Springs, CO: David C. Cook, 2014), 21.

CHAPTER 3
PRAYER PRINCIPLE #1: HEALTH AND HEALING

1. Marie Davis, in communication with the author. Used with permission.

2. Chartease Crittendon, in communication with the author. Used with permission.

3. Brenda Jackett, in communication with the author. Used with permission.

4. Jack W. Hayford, "Kingdom Dynamics: Psalm 91:9, 10: A Promise of Divinely Protected Health," *The Spirit-Filled Life Bible* (Nashville, TN: Thomas Nelson, 1991), 833.

CHAPTER 4
PRINCIPLE #2: EDUCATIONAL EXCELLENCE AND DEVELOPMENT

1. Story used with permission.

2. Hayford, *The Spirit-Filled Life Bible*, 884.

3. In communication with the author. Testimonies shared with permission.

4. Jonathan Robinson, in communication with the author. Used with permission.

CHAPTER 7
PRAYER PRINCIPLE #5: SUPERNATURAL PROMOTION AND INFLUENCE

1. Bob Reccord, *Made to Count* (Nashville, TN: Thomas Nelson Publishers, 2004).

2. Meg Heron-Blake, "Was Einstein Learning Disabled?," Learning Disabilities Association of Illinois, accessed February 19, 2015, http://www.ldail.com/index.php?option=com_content&view=article&id=32:einstein&catid=14&Itemid=117; Marlin Thomas, "Albert Einstein: An Evaluation of the Evidence," *Journal of Learning Disabilities* 33, no. 2 (March 2000): 149–157.

3. Ibid.

4. Author heard Reinhard Bonnke share this story during an evangelistic crusade in Lagos, Nigeria, in November 2000.

CONCLUSION
IT WORKS!

1. Sherry Lowery, in communication with the author. Used with permission.

.

EMPOWERED
TO RADICALLY CHANGE
YOUR WORLD

Charisma House brings you books, e-books, and other media from dynamic Spirit-filled Christians who are passionate about God.

Check out all of our releases from best-selling authors like **Jentezen Franklin**, **Perry Stone**, and **Kimberly Daniels** and experience God's supernatural power at work.

CHARISMA
HOUSE

www.charismahouse.com
twitter.com/charismahouse • facebook.com/charismahouse

11843

SUBSCRIBE TODAY

Exclusive Content

Inspiring Messages

Encouraging Articles

Discovering Freedom

CHARISMA MEDIA

FREE NEWSLETTERS

to experience the power of the *Holy Spirit*

Charisma Magazine Newsletter
Get top-trending articles, Christian teachings, entertainment reviews,
videos, and more.

Charisma News Weekly
Get the latest breaking news from an evangelical perspective
every Monday.

SpiritLed Woman
Receive amazing stories, testimonies, and articles on marriage,
family, prayer, and more.

New Man
Get articles and teaching about the realities of living in the world
today as a man of faith.

3-in-1 Daily Devotionals
Find personal strength and encouragement with these devotionals,
and begin your day with God's Word.

Sign up for Free at nl.charismamag.com